T0277192

BEYOND BELIEF, BEYOND CONSCIENCE

INALIENABLE RIGHTS SERIES

. . .

SERIES EDITOR
Geoffrey R. Stone

Stephen J. Schulhofer
ROBERT B. MCKAY PROFESSOR OF LAW
NEW YORK UNIVERSITY SCHOOL OF LAW

Geoffrey R. Stone
EDWARD H. LEVI DISTINGUISHED SERVICE
PROFESSOR
UNIVERSITY OF CHICAGO LAW SCHOOL

David A. Strauss
GERALD RATNER DISTINGUISHED SERVICE
PROFESSOR OF LAW
UNIVERSITY OF CHICAGO LAW SCHOOL

Kathleen M. Sullivan
STANLEY MORRISON PROFESSOR OF LAW
STANFORD LAW SCHOOL

Cass R. Sunstein
ROBERT WALMSLEY UNIVERSITY PROFESSOR
HARVARD LAW SCHOOL

Laurence H. Tribe
CARL M. LOEB UNIVERSITY
PROFESSOR OF LAW
HARVARD LAW SCHOOL

Mark V. Tushnet
WILLIAM NELSON CROMWELL
PROFESSOR OF LAW
HARVARD LAW SCHOOL

J. Harvie Wilkinson III
JUDGE
U.S. COURT OF APPEALS FOR THE FOURTH
CIRCUIT

Kenji Yoshino
CHIEF JUSTICE EARL WARREN PROFESSOR OF
CONSTITUTIONAL LAW
NEW YORK UNIVERSITY SCHOOL OF LAW

GEOFFREY STONE AND OXFORD UNIVERSITY PRESS GRATEFULLY ACKNOWLEDGE THE INTEREST AND SUPPORT OF THE FOLLOWING ORGANIZATIONS IN THE INALIENABLE RIGHTS SERIES: THE ALA; THE CHICAGO HUMANITIES FESTIVAL; THE AMERICAN BAR ASSOCIATION; THE NATIONAL CONSTITUTION CENTER; THE NATIONAL ARCHIVES

# Beyond Belief, Beyond Conscience

## The Radical Significance of the Free Exercise of Religion

Jack N. Rakove

OXFORD
UNIVERSITY PRESS

# OXFORD
UNIVERSITY PRESS

Oxford University Press is a department of the University of Oxford. It furthers
the University's objective of excellence in research, scholarship, and education
by publishing worldwide. Oxford is a registered trade mark of Oxford University
Press in the UK and certain other countries.

Published in the United States of America by Oxford University Press
198 Madison Avenue, New York, NY 10016, United States of America.

Library of Congress Cataloging-in-Publication Data
Names: Rakove, Jack N., 1947– author.
Title: Beyond belief, beyond conscience : the radical significance of
the free exercise of religion / Jack N. Rakove.
Description: New York : Oxford University Press, 2020. |
Series: Inalienable rights | Includes index.
Identifiers: LCCN 2019053105 (print) | LCCN 2019053106 (ebook) |
ISBN 9780195305814 (hardback) | ISBN 9780190086572 (epub) |
Subjects: LCSH: Freedom of religion—United States.
Classification: LCC KF4783 .R35 2020 (print) |
LCC KF4783 (ebook) | DDC 342.7308/52—dc23
LC record available at https://lccn.loc.gov/2019053105
LC ebook record available at https://lccn.loc.gov/2019053106

1 3 5 7 9 8 6 4 2
Printed by LSC Communications, United States of America

*For Stephen Scharf*
*My brother-in-law of blessed memory*
*and for*
*Leslie*
*Sophie, Matteo, and Luca*
*Sarah and Pat*

# Contents

. . .

# Editor's Note

. . .

We hold these truths to be self-evident, that all men are created
equal, that they are endowed by their Creator with certain unalienable Rights.

*—The Declaration of Independence*

In *Beyond Belief, Beyond Conscience*, Stanford History and Political
Science Professor and Pulitzer Prize winner Jack Rakove addresses
what he describes as "the radical significance of the free exercise of
religion." In this brilliant work, Rakove explores the evolution of
"religious freedom" from the sixteenth century to the modern era.
Rakove begins with a brief description of James Madison's declaration in 1776 that what a free society needs is a broad recognition
that "all men are equally entitled to the free exercise of religion,"
and with Madison's and Thomas Jefferson's joint commitment to
the principle that the free exercise of religion is a natural right that
the state could not abridge. In this gripping work, Rakove dedicates
himself to explaining "the enduring appeal of their approach."

To set the stage for Madison's and Jefferson's enduring contribution, Rakove turns back the clock and vividly depicts a world in

which tolerance of religious difference was seen as incompatible with the security of the state. The expulsion of the Jews from Spain in 1492 and the flight of the French Huguenots in 1685 are just two of many examples Rakove discusses. The greatest challenge of this era, though, was the slaughter by Christians of each other.

Crossing the Atlantic, Rakove next turns his attention to the American colonies. As he explains, "a principled belief in religious freedom as a right to be extended to all was *not* a value" that the colonists brought with them from Britain. Indeed, into the early decades of the eighteenth century, "religious dissent" in most of the colonies was seen as "a form of disease" that the authorities were morally obligated to suppress.

Rakove then focuses on the extraordinary fifteen-year period from 1776 to 1791, which he describes as "Jefferson's and Madison's Great Project." At the outset, Rakove notes that "the pursuit of religious liberty was not a part of the revolutionary movement that led to independence," but that by the end of this period "rethinking the religion problem" had become a "crucial facet" of efforts to define the meaning of liberty. In a truly fascinating account, Rakove traces the complex process by which Madison and Jefferson brought religious liberty to the very forefront of public debate, resulting ultimately in the ratification of the First Amendment to the Constitution.

Turning to the nineteenth century, Rakove then explores the impact of the Second Great Awakening, which reflected the "dawn of an evangelical age" in which Americans were "more religious than their colonial antecedents had been." The release of "spiritual energy" in this era led to the "creation of the 'moral establishment'" that led to prosecutions for blasphemy based on the conviction that "Christianity was the source of the moral convictions that informed American law." Another manifestation of this era focused on public education and on the demand that because "the Bible remained a universal source of human morality," all schoolchildren from an early age "should be properly instructed in its profound truths." This led to divisive disputes over the appropriate role of religion in public education. Rakove brings these and related controversies to life in a vibrant and engaging manner.

But what does the First Amendment mean in practice? How does the Supreme Court's jurisprudence comport with the intentions and understandings of Madison and Jefferson? Rakove focuses in particular on one of the most vexing First Amendment issues of our time: When does one's religious belief give one a right not to comply with a general law that is not directed at religion? As Rakove demonstrates, this is a long-standing puzzle, going back to the Court's 1879 decision in *Reynolds v. United States*, which held that the First Amendment did not give a member of the Mormon church the right to engage in polygamy in violation of federal law. As Rakove demonstrates, over the years the Court has gone back and forth on this question, reflecting the complexity of the very notion of "freedom of religion." In the end, Rakove proposes an approach to resolving this question, which he terms *Madison's razor*. I will leave it to the reader to figure out what that means.

This is a truly wonderful book, and it is a great honor for me to include it in the *Inalienable Rights* series.

Geoffrey R. Stone

2020

# Preface

· · ·

Some time back in the early 2000s, when—thanks to Dean John Sexton, my good friends Larry Kramer and John Ferejohn, and other colleagues—I used to hang out at New York University Law School, I had lunch one day with Dedi Felman, who was then a legal editor at Oxford University Press. We discussed her idea of doing a series of short provocative books on problems of rights in American constitutional history. When Geoffrey Stone of the University of Chicago (my literal birthplace) took over editing the Unalienable Rights series that Dedi organized, I quickly staked a claim to the Free Exercise Clause of the First Amendment. This interest reflected a longstanding concern with James Madison, dating to my dissertation work in the early 1970s, and other projects I had pursued since, including the problem of how one discusses the original meaning of the Constitution. The idea of religious freedom was a seminal element in the development of Madison's constitutional ideas. Equally important, the two components of the Religion Clause illustrated two landmark aspects of American constitutional practice. The free exercise of religion is a right different from all other rights because of the degree of moral autonomy it invests in each and every one of us. And the principle of disestablishment, by depriving the state of the power of regulating religion, offers the best example of the basic idea that the legislative authority government exercises depends on the will of a sovereign people.

These are points we do not readily grasp. In part because contemporary Religion Clause jurisprudence is such a messy and vexed subject, and in part because justices and judges often prefer resolving claims of conscience on general grounds of freedom of speech, this original significance of "the religion question" often escapes attention. The subtitle of this book rests on my conviction that a historically grounded approach to this subject would be of some value to legal scholars. Among other things, that approach involves asking how we should compare the gradual development of European modes of religious tolerance with the emerging American conviction that the free exercise of religion is no longer a matter of mere toleration.

A near decade and a half and the publication of several other books separated my joining the Unalienable Rights project and the completion of this book. The series has flourished while I was doing other things, but even so, I am very grateful that Geof Stone and David McBride, Dedi Felman's successor, have exercised another form of toleration while awaiting my manuscript. I have benefited from being able to present my ideas in lectures and workshops at Boston College, Notre Dame University, the United States Studies Centre at Sydney University (then run by my college classmate and current colleague, the fabulous political scientist Margaret Levi), Monash University, the University of Arkansas, the University of Southern California, and last but definitely not least, the Political Theory Seminar at Stanford, where Jackie Basu admirably critiqued my work, which may not have been the easiest challenge for my former senior thesis advisee. An invitation to chair the opening panel at a Harvard Law School conference on Religious Accommodation in the Age of Civil Rights was a terrific opportunity for me to learn a lot about doctrine from an impressive phalanx of legal scholars. Teaching this subject several times to Stanford students in my Heretics to Headscarves colloquium was a lot of fun; so was the opportunity to do a class on American religious freedom at the Hebrew University in Jerusalem law school in 2015.

The interpretive emphases in this book are obviously my own, but in other respects it is also very much a synthesis of a rich body of literature. I owe intellectual debts to a great fellowship of scholars, and special debts to two friends in particular: Carolyn Chappell Lougee of Stanford, for her careful reading of the first chapter, and her insistence that I be consistent in maintaining the crucial (if sometimes blurred) distinction between toleration and tolerance; and Chip Lupu of George Washington University law school, for his willingness to save me from many errors I might have wantonly inflicted on modern constitutional jurisprudence. Saying thanks to Chip is also a special pleasure because he and my wife, Helen, were K-12 schoolmates in Albany, New York. An annual conversation or two with Denis Lacorne of Sciences Po has offered a great way to think about the great comparison between the American system of religious freedom and that strange entity the French know as *laïcité*.

A substantial part of this book was written during my second sojourn at the Center for Advanced Study in the Behavioral Sciences in 2016–2017, a memorable year that began with the Cubs winning the pennant and the World Series, and which only got better (at least intellectually) after that. It was a great group of fellows to hang with, and once again a tribute is owed to Margaret Levi, who has done heroic work giving CASBS its new identity.

This book is dedicated to the blessed memory of my late brother-in-law, Stephen Scharf, whose own religious interests underwent a remarkable transformation in his junior year abroad trip around the world in 1970–1971, and also to his family. It is a remarkable comment on the nature of religious freedom in the United States that our two families, Rakove and Scharf, solidly Ashkenazi in their origins, now have intimate links to Britain, Korea, Italy, and Thailand. Following the logic of John Locke, which I invoke several times in this book, I leave it to my two grandsons, Alexander Taeyoung Rakove and Elliot Milton Rakove, to choose their own religious identities or even to abandon that choice altogether. That decision is a fundamental aspect of the religious liberty that we have inherited from our history and a right we should proudly assert.

# Introduction
## The View from Montpelier and Monticello

"WE ARE TEACHING the world the great truth that Governments do better without Kings & Nobles than with them," James Madison observed in 1822. "The merit will be doubled by the other lesson that Religion flourishes in greater purity, without than with the aid of Govt."[1] This lesson confirmed views he had long held. Half a century earlier, as a graduate of the College of New Jersey (now Princeton University), he had returned to Montpelier, the family plantation outside Orange, Virginia, imbued with a deep commitment to religious freedom. When local magistrates arrested half a dozen itinerant Baptists in a neighboring county for preaching without a license, the young Madison railed against the narrow prejudices of the established clergy who pressed the charges (a "Quota of Imps," he called them). "I have squabbled and scolded abused and ridiculed so long about it, to so little purpose that I am without common patience," he wrote his college friend Billy Bradford, who later became the nation's second attorney general.[2]

Yet beneath these snide comments about his rustic neighbors lay a set of principles that were formative to Madison's constitutional ideals and reflective of the emerging American approach to religious liberty. Madison was no mere tolerationist. He did not regard religious freedom merely as a legal privilege that the state could grant its subjects but also revoke—as Louis XIV had famously annulled the Edict of Nantes in 1685, stripping French Huguenots of the legal protection they had enjoyed since 1598. Freedom of conscience and the public expression of religious beliefs were natural rights that every individual owned, just as they owned their property. These were not mere procedural rights, nurtured in the common-law tradition, requiring the government to apply fixed and fair standards in dealing with its subjects. The free exercise of religion treated each member of society, male and female, as morally autonomous individuals who could make fundamental choices that the state had no ability to regulate. Religious freedom was the most liberal right of all, the one that placed the greatest value on the subjective moral independence of individuals.

So, too, Madison's support for disestablishment—for the severance of formal relations between church and state and the end of public subsidies to religion—marked a second and equally important constitutional commitment. This was the idea that the powers that government wielded were not derived from the inherent authority of the state, but rather arose from positive acts of delegation from a sovereign people. The idea that there were formal limits on the authority of the state—that there were areas of human activity that its lawmaking power could not reach—would have made little sense in the eighteenth century, except at the most abstract levels of political theory.[3] But the idea of removing religion from the realm of public regulation and support marked the first area where the state could be denied the authority to legislate at all. Prudence alone would have dictated that no state could abjure its authority to regulate religion—a realm of human activity that was simply too important, and often too dangerous, to ignore. But in Madison's view, that authority was indeed a power that society should not and need not delegate to government. Religion was a wholly private matter, a duty to be discharged by autonomous individuals and the voluntary religious associations (call them churches, synagogues, congregations, or meetings) where worshippers gathered

As a young man of the Revolution, a person whose career began only when British rule collapsed in 1774, Madison seized the opportunity to act on these principles when he attended the Fifth Provincial Convention that met at Williamsburg in May 1776. There he served on the committee that wrote a constitution and declaration of rights for the Commonwealth of Virginia. As originally proposed, the religion article in the Declaration of Rights was a statement of the principle of toleration. Madison, just turned twenty-five, wanted something more: a broad recognition that "all men are equally entitled to the free exercise of religion." With support from key political elders, Madison carried the point. Freedom of religion was no longer a legal privilege extended by the state, but a right that all of its citizens possessed.

When Madison returned to Williamsburg in the fall of 1776 to attend the new House of Delegates, he joined its committee on religion. Here he met Thomas Jefferson from neighboring Albemarle County, launching the acquaintance that became the greatest friendship in American political history. The committee's chief duty was to consider the petitions favoring disestablishment of the Church of England that were flooding the assembly, inspired in part by the bold language of Madison's amended religion article. On this question, as on so many others, the two men were of one mind. Both treated the free exercise of religion as a natural right that the state could not abridge. Both wanted to sever the formal legal ties between church and state. And both grasped the historical novelty of their position.

Jefferson put the point directly in the reading notes he compiled while staying at the home of George Wythe, his law teacher at the College of William and Mary. Commenting on a key passage in John Locke's *Letter Concerning Toleration*, Jefferson observed that "It was a great thing to go so far (as he himself sais of the parl[iament] who framed the act of toler[atio]n)" of 1689; "but where he stopped short, we may go on."[4]

For Jefferson and Madison, *going on* soon involved writing some of the landmark texts of American religious liberty: the Virginia Statute for Religious Freedom, drafted by Jefferson in the late 1770s and enacted with Madison's active guidance in 1786; the *Memorial and Remonstrance against Religious Assessments* that Madison drafted in 1785; the chapter on religious history in Jefferson's *Notes on the State of Virginia*; the initial and final versions of the Religion Clause of the First Amendment; Jefferson's 1802 letter to the Baptists of Danbury, Connecticut, promoting a wall of separation between church and state; and other documents that elaborate their joint commitment. These texts have generated a hefty body of scholarship and exerted seminal influence over judicial interpretations of the Religion Clause. This attention is well deserved, and not only because of their respective roles in drafting the Declaration of Independence, the Constitution, and the Bill of Rights. On the religion question, Jefferson and Madison marked the advanced edge of American thinking. They may not have been the most representative commentators on this issue. Nor should one treat the American commitment to free exercise as a simple byproduct of their ideas. Yet given their exceptional relevance to the American political tradition, their concerns remain a necessary element in the origins of this fundamental constitutional norm.

To explain why the two Virginians valued this right so highly also requires us to ask why the religion problem had an importance for them that it has since lost. One can only perform that task by thinking historically, that is, by describing the contexts within which this commitment emerged. That means that this book will be less concerned with critiquing judicial notions of religious freedom than with exploring how ideas and behavior have shaped the unique configuration of constitutional values and religious practice that distinguishes the United States from other relevantly comparable nations. That distinction rests on two conditions. First, the United States is remarkable for its radical version of disestablishment—that is, for the complete absence of public support for the maintenance of religious doctrines and institutions. Second, in postrevolutionary America religious activity accordingly took place within an unregulated spiritual marketplace where rival faiths and denominations competed to capture the faith and allegiance of ordinary truth-seekers, making Americans the most religious society in the industrial world. This combination of public disestablishment with private zeal is what has set the United States apart. These two conditions were mutually supportive. Disestablishment provided the incentive that inspired and indeed required faiths and denominations to compete, and the working success of the free exercise of religion made establishment redundant or superfluous. Taken together, these two conditions fulfilled Madison's mature vision of the benefits of the American approach, proving that "Religion flourishes in greater purity, without than with the aid of Government."

There are, of course, other modes of exploring the content and character of this commitment to the free exercise of religion. As is usually the case in constitutional scholarship, the dominant approach treats judicial decision-making and the evolution of legal doctrine as the most valuable perspective and source. But describing what this means in practice is no easy task. It takes a painstaking survey of legal decisions, fraught with many qualifications and distinctions, to make sense of modern Religion Clause doctrine.[5] For many commentators the net result of such a survey is to produce an abiding

[ 5 ]

dismay not only with the perceived shortcomings of so many decisions but also with the general incoherence of the doctrine, insofar
as it actually exists.

In response to that perception, numerous legal scholars have
struggled valiantly to offer their own preferred solutions to the
defects of judicial doctrine, attempting to survey the existing corpus to produce the one best account of what that doctrine should
be. Their ranks include an impressive array of prominent academic
authorities, and one could organize quite an interesting seminar
based simply on their leading books.[b]

Historians can contribute to this effort by criticizing the errors
that jurists and legal commentators make as they mine the historical record, prospecting a useful cite here or there. But they can
hardly be expected to improve the legal doctrine. Such an endeavor
lies beyond their intellectual competence and professional qualifications. The best contribution that historians can make lies elsewhere: to explain how the quandaries of Religion Clause doctrine
are not merely functions of differences in judicial thinking or ideological commitments, but rather reflect conditions and tensions
embodied in our historical experience.

Such a historically grounded account would include the following objectives.

First, if Jefferson, Madison, and their revolutionary contemporaries understood that they were going beyond a European regime
of toleration, it might be helpful to ask how, why, and when the
European practice of tolerance and the American movement toward
the free exercise of religion diverged. Such a comparison involves
something more than contrasting ideas of toleration and free exercise.
That comparison is relatively easy to make. The greater challenge
is to explain how European societies and individual communities
slowly developed working practices of religious tolerance, when toleration retained its traditional meaning of begrudgingly accepting

burdens that were deemed abhorrent and detestable. Seventeenth- and eighteenth-century Europeans did not develop modes of tolerance because they discovered sympathetic feelings toward their dissident countrymen, whom they often disparaged as deviant and dissolute libertines. Rather, they reluctantly accepted toleration because the costs of maintaining religious uniformity had grown too high. Many American colonists shared this disdain for religious dissenters. Yet by the middle of the eighteenth century—before Jefferson and Madison entered the scene—Americans were already accepting the norms of free exercise. To understand why progress in Europe came with so many difficulties while the American story proved much simpler marks the real point of comparison.

Second, the success of that story was not a simple matter of enlightened colonists readily accepting freedom of conscience as a natural, universally endowed right. The religious liberty they initially sought was meant to protect their own versions of faith, not to open the floodgates of sectarian competition. When obnoxious dissenters appeared, like the radical Quakers who pestered seventeenth-century New England, civil authorities had every right to prosecute, even execute, these zealots. Yet over time the colonists generally agreed that denominations should be free to disseminate their spiritual messages and that individuals were competent to pick their religious affiliations. The sectarian competition released by the mid-eighteenth-century Great Awakening was one source of this shift in attitudes. But so, at a deeper level, was the radical emphasis that New England Puritans had long placed on the experience of conversion (the faithful rebirth in Jesus). That emphasis was not shared by every other Protestant denomination. But its prominent presence in American religious experience and the debates it sparked required ordinary men and women to agonize over the state of their souls, and to ask which denomination best answered their spiritual craving for salvation. The lively presence of this radical

Protestantism gave individuals a powerful incentive to assert their rights of conscience, making free exercise a value they commonly treasured. By the eve of the Revolution, a commitment to this form of religious freedom permeated American society, and the leaders of most denominations understood that they were already competing with their rivals to gather adherents.

Third, it was against the background of this social and cultural experience that Jefferson and Madison articulated their program of reform. The opportunity that independence created—to write republican constitutions and codes of law—also became an occasion to confront the religion question directly, and to link its solution to their larger project of political innovation. Jefferson was one of the first to grasp the problem of distinguishing a written constitution from ordinary statutory law. The concluding paragraph of his Bill for Religious Freedom explicitly recognized the inadequacy of grounding the protection of a fundamental natural right on a mere statutory basis, because a later legislature with improper intentions could always undo the good work of a previous session. For Madison, the matter of religious freedom represented the paradigmatic example of the potential tyranny of a popular majority over a minority. In conventional eighteenth-century thinking, the problem of rights had been to protect the people as a whole against the concentrated authority of a monarchical state. By contrast, in the new republics of revolutionary America, the true challenge was to protect the rights of minorities and individuals against the collective will of the majority, acting through the legislative power of the state. For these reasons and others, the protection of religious freedom was not merely one right among many; it was instead intimately tied to broader conceptions of constitutional change.

Fourth, the acceptance of the principles of free exercise and disestablishment contributed to the birth of the postrevolutionary spiritual marketplace that accompanied the Second Great

Awakening. This was the epoch of hothouse religious competition that Nathan Hatch has characterized as *The Democratization of American Christianity*, emphasizing the parallels between American attitudes to religious and political authority. But this response was itself complicated. In religiously orthodox circles and especially among the Calvinists of New England—the reaction against the turmoil of the French Revolution and the popularity of freethinkers like Thomas Paine reinforced the traditional belief that religion was so essential a source of civic virtue that it still merited active support from the state. Equally important, the success of evangelical Christianity fostered the creation of a "moral establishment" in which overtly Protestant values continued to suffuse American law. There are numerous examples of how this moral establishment operated: the campaign to block Sunday mail delivery, the rise of the temperance movement to correct the vices of a postrevolutionary "alcoholic republic," the denial of the right to testify to witnesses who did not believe in divine judgment in the world to come, the nonsectarian reading of the King James Bible in the schools as a source of universal moral authority. But the creation of this moral and legal establishment in turn sparked its own opposition.[7] Other Americans, relying on Jeffersonian principles, argued that the United States needed a "second disestablishment" to renew and complete the project of the first. Together, the opposition between these two sets of aspirations and commitments illuminated the ways in which the concerns and quandaries that still vex us were embedded in the structures of religious and civic practice.

All of these factors form the deep background—a historical prologue or prolegomenon, if you will—to the current state of free exercise doctrine. The real development of that doctrine is largely a twentieth- and twenty-first-century phenomenon. It pivots on some celebrated judicial decisions, notably including the Flag Salute cases (1940 and 1943), *Sherbert v. Verner* (1963),[8] *Wisconsin v. Yoder* (1971),[9] and *Oregon Employment Division v. Smith* (1990);[10] the passage of the Religious Freedom Restoration Act (1993) and the Religious Land Use and Institutionalized Persons Act (2000); and most recently, legal challenges to the Affordable Care Act of 2010 and the Supreme Court's decision legalizing same-sex marriage in *Obergefell v. Hodges* (2015).[11] The premise of these cases involves asking whether institutions and individuals can seek exemptions from statutes and regulations that would make them complicit in activities that violate their deeply felt religious convictions. The language of contemporary free exercise doctrine pivots on ideas of accommodation and exemption. At first glance, the advocates of accommodation and exemption are not concerned with the issues that troubled our ancestors. It is not the freedom to believe or disbelieve or to disseminate religious truths that troubles them.[12] Their concern lies instead with their legal obligation to comply with either the regulatory demands of the modern state or the egalitarian and nondiscriminatory norms that now shape our jurisprudence.

These are conditions and circumstances of governance that barely existed, if they existed at all, in the early modern era. Just as the activities of the modern regulatory state have expanded exponentially beyond the bounds of eighteenth-century governance, so, too, our conceptions of human equality have implications that even Thomas Jefferson, *primus inter pares*, never considered. As important as his and Madison's understanding of the free exercise of religion might be, it cannot supplant our own duty to puzzle out the difficulties we face on their own terms—even in an age of originalist jurisprudence. Readers of this brief and intentionally provocative work will not discover a fixed set of historical answers to our contemporary problems.

The deeper argument of this book lies elsewhere: in the proposition that the radical significance of the free exercise of religion inheres in its recognition of the moral autonomy of individuals, and

that this recognition marks the true beginning of the liberal project. That claim may seem surprising today, when claims about religious liberty are often subsumed within the broader framework of
freedom of speech. Precisely because judges have good reasons to
avoid making any judgments about the sincerity or content of religious convictions, theories of free speech provide a superior basis for
evaluating the array of claims that make their way into court.[13] But
historically the recognition of the freedom of religious expression
preceded the acceptance of more liberal ideas of free speech. The
relaxation of laws prohibiting blasphemy occurred before the liber-
alization of seditious libel; adults of both sexes enjoyed the opportunity to make a choice of religious vocation before they gained full
political rights as citizens. One could criticize one's minister more
easily than one's representative. The insulation of an individual's
interior realm of conscience from the scrutiny of the state was a seminal statement of a concept of privacy. So was the recognition, dating
to the parliamentary Conventicle Acts of the 1660s and 1670s, that
families could privately engage in religious practices that would be
outlawed in public.[14] One could plausibly argue that the best textual
source for a concept of constitutional privacy does not lie in the nebulous "penumbras, formed by emanations" from the Bill of Rights
that Justice William Douglas invoked in *Griswold v. Connecticut*[15] but
more directly in the Free Exercise Clause. The birth of the modern
self—or perhaps a subject we can also describe as a constitutional
self—originally owed more to the realm of religion than it did to
politics. The radical significance of the free exercise of religion thus
rests not only on its seminal contribution to individual moral autonomy, but also upon the ways in which it formulated crucial aspects
of American constitutionalism.

Historians may not always believe that there are lessons of the
past that can be readily applied to contemporary situations. The real
challenge of the study of history is to distinguish past from present,

not to narrow the differences between them. Nor is it our real intellectual duty to judge the misdeeds of past actors from the ostensibly superior moral vantage point of the present. Like Jefferson and Madison, one can readily find much to condemn in the horrors that religious convictions and prejudices long perpetrated and continue to inflict to this day. But moral condemnation is an easy task; historical explanation is a much more difficult endeavor. Here, too, historians and lawyers often speak in different voices (though admittedly many historians do express moral commitments in their writings). Yet in this instance, I find much to admire and emulate in the approach to the religion problem that Jefferson and Madison mounted, and this book will, in part, try to explain the enduring appeal of their convictions.

## CHAPTER ONE

# The Burden of Toleration

A GREAT AND happy irony accompanies the benefit of living, as
Americans rightly believe they do, in a society that actively practices religious tolerance. In such a society, one no longer needs to
know what religious toleration originally meant. Indeed, the need
to distinguish an idea or policy of *toleration* from the attitudes and
practices that make *tolerance* possible is a problem that still challenges scholars. The two words are often used interchangeably, and
individual scholars wrestle with the proper definition. In general, we
might say that toleration involves explaining why religious diversity
should be accepted, as a matter of philosophy or public policy, while
tolerance is concerned with developing attitudes and behaviors that
preserve peace and a measure of harmony within a community.[1] For
our purposes, the key holding is that the experience of living within
a tolerant society makes a proper understanding of toleration more,
not less, difficult.

Historically, within the traditions of Western Christendom, the
concept of toleration and the practice of tolerance meant having to

shoulder an offensive burden. Both required the grudging acceptance of religious beliefs and practices that one found offensive or
insulting, disturbing or ludicrous. "To tolerate was not to recognize
or to grant equal rights to a rival system of belief," the English historian Alexandra Walsham observes; "it was to permit or license
something of which one emphatically disapproved, to make a mag-
nanimous concession to the adherents of an inherently false religion." Communities became tolerant not because they recognized
the moral rights of dissenters, but rather because the task of preserving religious uniformity through tested techniques of persecution
had grown too costly.[2]

Americans today may have to struggle to grasp the nuances
of this definition (just as we also puzzle to comprehend what the
French mean by *laïcité*, their term for the separation of state from
church that has no proper English translation). For us, tolerance is
a moderate virtue, something we learn easily in our schools, families, and many (though not all) of our religious communities. When
tolerance seems to totter—as it does in communities that worry
that *sharia* law will be imposed on them, or that the building of a
mosque poses some mortal danger to the flow of traffic, or that a
virtually invisible *eruv* will turn their homes into Jewish domestic
space, through some arcane kabbalistic feat—the prejudices of our
narrow-minded countrymen embarrass us. But we no longer regard
tolerance as self-imposed suffering. A tolerant society prides itself
on its liberal attitudes, and thus no longer knows what attaining this
happy condition once entailed. We project backward onto our colonial forebears the attitudes we cherish in ourselves, assuming that
their own sectarian quests for religious liberty naturally led them to
extend similar rights to other truth-seekers.

The real history is (as historians always like to say) more complicated. The early generations of colonists were not such enlightened liberals; they shared the assumptions of their countrymen

who stayed at home. One can understand the significance of the American acceptance of the free exercise of religion as a natural and constitutional right only if one first considers how Europeans developed principles of toleration and modes of tolerance. It is not enough to simply draw a contrast between the burdensome practice of toleration in post-Reformation Europe and a principled commitment to the free exercise of religion in enlightened America. One also has to ask what made this contrast possible, and why the critical American transition, when it did occur, came so easily.

To tell this story comprehensively would be a daunting task. Part of this history extends to the Christian treatment of infidels, that is, Jews, Moslems, and the indigenous American peoples whom European empires subordinated after 1500. That history—rich, complicated, and catastrophic as it is—will receive only passing mention here. These peoples lived, in a certain sense, beyond the boundaries of the Christian community, properly defined. How they related to their Christian and imperial governors is an important special subject in its own right, and one that does shed some light on the nature and limits of European ideas of religious toleration. The great Valladolid debate of 1550, when Bartolomé de las Casas, Juan Ginés de Sepúlveda, and other scholars debated the moral qualities of the indigenous American population, was a landmark moment in the development of both Spanish imperial policy and European ethnology.[3] Periodic debates between Jewish rabbis and Christian theologians marked a form of accommodation vastly superior to the pogroms, forced conversions, and expulsions that repeatedly plagued and decimated Jewish communities. At certain notable points—say, the medieval kingdoms of Iberia— the propinquity of two or all three of the Abrahamic faiths in one space illustrates how working practices of tolerance could arise from the circumstances of daily life. The folk belief that "each can be saved in his own faith" without having to accept the truths of

Christianity was a common heresy that the Catholic Inquisition strove to suppress.[4]

Nevertheless, the ideas and practices of toleration that matter most to us largely derive from the disputes that Christians had with each other. This story is primarily about matters of heresy, blasphemy, orthodoxy, dissent, skepticism, the number and identity of the sacraments, doctrines of baptism and transubstantiation, the regulation of "indifferent" matters (*adiophora*), and the fundamental choice between Trinitarian dogma and Unitarian (or Socinian) convictions. This Christian story arguably has a doctrinal and philosophical complexity that the legalistic and liturgical emphases of Judaism and Islam lack. But core elements and tenets of Christian faith—the divinity of Jesus, the puzzle of the crucifixion and resurrection of god as man, original sin, the relation between baptism and infant damnation, the mystery of transubstantiation, philosophical proofs of the existence of God—generated endless unresolvable disputes that ensured the inherent divisiveness of Christianity. Before the sixteenth century, the Church of Rome kept these centrifugal forces largely in check. But once Martin Luther precipitated the Reformation, the emergence of confessional Christianity in the sixteenth and seventeenth centuries made the quest for individual religious freedom a controlling problem of governance, politics, and, finally, the invention of the natural or constitutional right of religious freedom.

UNEVEN PATHS TOWARD TOLERANCE

The traditional history of religious toleration has been a matter of great writers and influential texts, really a history of ideas. The starting point for this story necessarily has to explain the doctrinal sources of religious *intolerance*, the prior condition that had to be overcome. This history dates to late antiquity—to the conversion of the emperor Constantine to Christianity, to the Council of Nicaea of 325 and its promulgation of doctrinal orthodoxy, and especially to the legacy of St. Augustine of Hippo (354–430), Christianity's supreme theologian. Augustine's interpretation of the phrase *compelle intrare* (Gospel of Luke, 14: 23) in the parable of the wealthy man whose guests shirked his invitation to dinner became the foundational text for the idea that the church had legitimate authority to apply coercive physical measures against religious dissenters and heretics. That verse was commonly invoked to justify physical means of compelling obstinate dissidents to consider theological arguments they would otherwise ignore or reject. Admittedly, force alone could not produce a change of conscience, because conscience was a matter of inner conviction. Artful dissidents could always perform observable acts of conformity while masking their interior doubts. They could also apply modes of dissimulation to disguise their true convictions.[5] But coercive measures could at least generate a spiritual conversation that would never occur otherwise. If individuals balked at listening to corrective arguments, their perseverance would lead not to acts of mercy granted in respect of their devotion, but to greater coercion still. But this coercion was conceived not as an act of terror but as a benefit. This is why, Walsham remarks, the decision "to persecute was to display a charitable hatred," because the real charity lay in the desire to relieve the dissident of his heretical (and therefore damning) beliefs. Yet the decision to tolerate was equally a form of charitable hatred, because now charity inhered in the act of allowing dissidents to retain convictions one still despised. Persecution and tolerance were not binary choices or dialectical opposites, Walsham persuasively argues; they were instead intimately bound to each other.

The seminal advocates of religious toleration include such luminaries as Montaigne, John Milton, Benedictus (*née* Baruch) Spinoza,

John Locke, Pierre Bayle, and Voltaire, and the catalog of relevant works is even longer. Arguably the single most important work in this tradition was Bayle's great philosophical foray refuting the standard Augustinian doctrine of *compelle intrare*.[6] The writings of Sebastian Castellio, who has been described as "the first champion of religious toleration," also merit special attention.[7] Within the Anglo-American tradition, however, the dominant text is Locke's *Epistola de Tolerantia* (in the English translation, *A Letter Concerning Toleration*, prepared by William Popple).[8] The evolution of ideas of toleration can be told with relative economy or in enormously close detail.[9] But this approach to the subject remains throughout a saga of the movement and elaboration of ideas.

Could lasting conditions of religious tolerance ever exist if philosophical writers did not articulate a persuasive rationale for toleration? Arguably they could not. The alternative path available to rulers was to pursue the prudent path known in sixteenth-century France as *politique*, a calculated policy of toleration that would operate only so long as the security of the state demanded coexistence between rival faiths. When the state decided that those conditions no longer held, tolerance could come to a dramatic end. The expulsion of the Jews from Spain in 1492 and the dragooning, persecution, and flight of the French Huguenots with the Revocation of the Edict of Nantes in 1685 appear as harbingers of modern totalitarianism and the tyrannical denial of human rights. Yet as architects of the modern nation-state, Ferdinand and Isabella and Louis XIV thought they were pursuing wholly sensible policies of unifying their countries by having their subjects adhere to one faith. *Un roi, une loi, une foi*—one king, one law, one faith—was a highly compelling idea and a harbinger of modern nationalism.

Attaining conditions of lasting tolerance posed a far more difficult challenge, both politically and intellectually. Just as the forging of coherent legal doctrines depends on authoritative judicial deci-sions or legislative acts, so toleration in the robust sense of the term requires a principled commitment capable of transcending and with-standing the passions of the moment. Permanent religious liberty needs a philosophically compelling statement of its principles the kind of intellectual "work" that Spinoza, Locke, and Bayle set out to do in the late seventeenth century, and which Jefferson and Madison echoed a century later.[10]

Yet if principled arguments for religious toleration form a *neces-sary* cause of its lasting establishment, those arguments alone hardly provide a *sufficient* explanation of its existence. It could not be the case that the leaders of different societies awoke one day, opened their copies of Locke's *Epistola* (in its original Latin), and promptly imbibed its conclusions. Tolerance is as much a matter of behavior as of belief. It is a problem of neighbors learning (or relearning) how to live with each other; of cities, towns, and villages discovering how to share their churches, streets, and cemeteries; of finding ways to avoid the incivilities and confrontations, often involving trivial incidents, that could spark sudden eruptions of communal violence.

The study of patterns of communal behavior that fostered work-ing conditions of tolerance has thus marked an important innova-tion in recent historical writings. Benjamin Kaplan's excellent book, *Divided by Faith*, describes an array of practices that Europeans developed to make tolerance possible.[11] Tolerance emerged within a world where religious obligations and exercises had deeply pub-lic dimensions, for they were intimately interwoven with the daily life of the community—a *corpus Christianum* whose moral fabric and social integrity were rudely violated by the expression of religious dissent. Holy days and saints days were communal events, and ignoring or disrupting their performance, as Protestants grew wont to do, diluted essential bonds of community.[12]

Consider the recurring practice of parading the Host—the Eucharistic wafer that Catholics believe becomes the very body of Christ through transubstantiation, just as communion wine becomes his blood. When priests carried the Host down the street, Catholics routinely knelt and doffed their hats, but Protestants balked at imitating their neighbors. Sometimes they ducked down alleyways, only to find priests scurrying after them in an attempt to corner and expose them. The public singing of confessional songs was another source of confrontation. So were the rigid Sabbatarianism that many Protestants practiced and their avoidance of saints' days that had long functioned as sources of relaxation for the entire community. Adherence to a Protestant calendar in a Catholic-dominated town— or vice versa—threatened communal integrity from within. Popular attitudes therefore often treated dissenters, whether Protestant or Catholic, as potential fifth columnists or worse, a venomous presence within the communal body.[13]

Under these conditions, casual contacts and verbal exchanges in streets and squares could escalate into outright confrontations that soon led to one form of violence or another: violence against religious sites, fist-fights and beatings, or open riots that led to the loss of life. Protestants were more inclined to commit violence against objects—they were the great iconoclasts, after all—and Catholics against persons. Three types of occurrences were especially provocative, Kaplan argues: "processions, holiday celebrations, and funerals."[14] These created the "flashpoints" when residents who knew each other quite well became Reformation equivalents of the Montagues and Capulets. A simple incident of misbehavior or defiance, randomly sparked by some personal provocation, some sharp insult or incivility, could escalate into violent confrontations that revealed just how elusive the practice of tolerance must be.

These were the obstacles that communities had to overcome to make tolerance work or at least to prune the fruits of intolerance.

Kaplan describes several innovations that pursued this end. One was the practice of *Auslauf*, the term used to describe the Sunday journeys of Viennese Protestants to neighboring communities where they could worship as they wished. Thousands would leave Vienna in this way, and similar practices were followed in other communities. The sixteenth-century doctrine of *cuius regio, eius religio* (whose region, his religion), when applied in the multiple small jurisdictions of central Europe, meant that religious minorities could vote with their feet to pursue their faith. The only catch was that migrants had to go quietly, without singing their hymns or engaging in other triumphalist expressions. A different practice was the construction of the *schuilkerk*, an interior chapel built within the confines of much larger buildings, where dissenters could worship freely—but also quietly, so that passersby in the street would not hear their services. These sites enjoyed a nominal secrecy—one had to know where to find them—but the key factor was that they were private, not public places of worship. A third variation occurred when Protestants and Catholics shared a village or a parish church or a cemetery. Here ways were found to allow the dominant majority and the dissenters to use a common space, by alternating the timing of services or by creating distinct areas of worship, one adorned in the Catholic manner, the other stripped bare to conform to Protestant sensibilities.[15]

These observations describe the general difficulties that Europeans faced in their efforts to solve the religion problem—that is, to find ways to stop Christians from killing each other, as they freely did during the slaughter of the Anabaptists in the 1530s; the French wars of religion of the late sixteenth century, including the horrifying St. Bartholomew's Day massacre of 1572; and the Thirty Years' War (1618–1648). Building conditions of toleration was a concern both of state policy and communal conciliation. From the governing realms of kingdoms and duchies all the way down the jurisdictional ladder to towns and villages, solving the religion problem remained a preeminent concern of public policy. It was a problem that could not be solved by renouncing the authority of the state over religion, or by recognizing an individual's autonomous right to practice whichever faith he or she preferred in any community where one resided. Religious truth-seekers could be allowed to migrate to friendlier jurisdictions, but they had no recognized right to pursue their faith against the wishes of government.

The existence of these moderating mechanisms, however, did little to soften the deep confessional tendencies at play in Reformation Europe, which worked to harden denominational lines and enhance sectarian identities. Ordinary churchgoers grew ever more knowledgeable and sophisticated about their sectarian doctrines and practices and ever more contemptuous of the positions of the other faith.[16] The frequent experience of martyrdom, vividly memorialized in sermons, songs, and tracts, as well as the visual images retained after so many public executions, had a similarly powerful effect.[17] The idea that "each can be saved in his own faith" might enjoy some limited success when Christians, Jews, and Moslems were neighbors, as in pre-1492 Iberia, but its liberating possibilities did not extend to conflicts among Christians. So, too, while Protestants of different confessions might intermarry, Protestant–Catholic marriages occurred much less frequently and proved much more disruptive of family relations.[18]

Attaining conditions of tolerance was thus a hard-to-earn process, and its achievements were often only limited in nature. It remained a policy that could be abandoned as easily as it could be advanced. No state would renounce its legal authority over religious matters in the name of securing the rights of all its subjects. Religion was too important a matter, too much an element of state policy, to be treated as a personal right that ordinary individuals simply or naturally possessed.

The classic act of abandonment came in 1685, when Louis XIV revoked the Edict of Nantes of 1598. That act of policy concluded roughly a century and a third of controversy and conflict that had led to unsteady phases of sectarian coexistence that required repeated negotiations to produce a tenuous religious peace. The Huguenot community was still officially called *la religion prétendue réformée* (the pretended or so-called Reformed religion), a marker of how tentative the movement toward religious peace had always been. The deterioration of Huguenot life in the 1680s was a brutal affair. Reformed households were subject to being dragooned, meaning that soldiers were quartered in Protestant homes at their owners' expense. Stories abound of soldiers abusing wives, daughters, and servants, selling the furnishings and the crops and the livestock, drinking their way through the wine cellar, and generally doing as much damage as they desired. Another punishment was imposed on Huguenot families: they could lose the custody of their children, who could be placed in Catholic families or institutions and reared within the official faith. The only solutions to this wanton violation of domestic peace were either forswearing one's religious loyalties and accepting the Church of Rome, or else planning an escape that risked leaving much of one's property behind.[19]

The revocation of the Edict concluded a quarter-century of worsening persecution that began with the full ascent of Louis XIV to the kingship in 1661. The years that followed brought the destruction of numerous Huguenot temples, the imposition of legal penalties on ordinary adherents, and the active use of military force and brutal violence to compel Huguenots to renounce their faith. After exile became the last option for those who wished neither to abjure their faith nor to live as masked Calvinists in a Catholic culture—like the "new Christian" Marranos of Iberia—refugee communities appeared in Holland, Britain, Prussia, and Switzerland. (Some families made their way to British North America: the third and fourth presidents of the Continental Congress, Henry Laurens and John Jay, claimed Huguenot descent). The very word *refugee*, which figures so prominently in the modern discourse of human rights, was invented to describe the Huguenot diaspora.[20]

To a modern eye, the persecution and exile of the Huguenots appear to exemplify the emergence of the idea of human rights. Their plight and fate, which were elaborately described in tracts and autobiographical writings, became a *cause célèbre* within the international Protestant community. In their negotiations with the French monarchy, the Huguenots repeatedly invoked the specific edicts and decrees that had promised to ensure their physical and religious safety. But on one specific matter they reinforced this appeal to points already conceded with a more general invocation of the fundamental natural right of parents to control their children's religious education. Under an edict of June 17, 1681, the monarchy allowed Huguenot children as young as seven to make a choice of religion and to be removed from their families and raised as Catholics. In a *Humble Address* to Louis XIV, Huguenots not only protested the conflict between this provision and other agreements dating to the Edict of Nantes. They also argued that it violated "a Law of Nature [which] is as ancient as the world (and 'tis a Maxim, that natural Rights are immutable)" as well as "the Custom of all Nations." Education could be said to begin only at age seven, the moment when "Parents do as it were take Possession of their Right" to rear their children in their own religion. Perhaps at fourteen children could "be left to their Choice and Liberty" in religious matters, but until then parents held a natural and civil right to exercise that duty.[21]

Of course, a vocabulary of human rights was not yet available in seventeenth-century political thinking. To treat the Huguenot exile, like the expulsion of the Iberian Jews, as a paradigmatic prototype of the invention of human rights would thus commit the sin that historians fear most: anachronism. In the Huguenot campaign to maintain a regime of toleration, desperate appeals to the natural rights of parents mattered far less than efforts to remind the French monarchy of the concessions it had previously offered. But a privilege or liberty that the state had granted was also a privilege or liberty it could revoke. The dominant model of statecraft (or statebuilding) preferred religious uniformity to religious pluralism.

Still, observations of the Huguenot experience did have a major impact on the development of tolerationist thinking. John Locke lived in France during the late 1670s, when he had ample contact with the Huguenot community. When he went into political exile in Holland a decade later, Huguenot refugees were present in large numbers. Pierre Bayle also took refuge in Holland, where he became embroiled in continuing controversies with his former patron, Pierre Jurieu, the great spokesman for Calvinist civil liberty. And Spinoza, the most famous of excommunicated Jews, was descended from the Iberian refugees, many of them "new Christians" and Marranos, who reclaimed their ancestral religious identity in Holland. For an abundance of reasons, Holland became one of the two national forums for the philosophical development of modern ideas of religious liberty. The other forum was England, to which Locke returned only after the Glorious Revolution of 1688 secured its existence as a Protestant realm.

### ENGLISH DISSENT AND A NEW MAGNA CARTA

England had conducted its own experiments in restoring religious uniformity. In its origins, the English Reformation of the 1530s was an act of state, driven by King Henry VIII's desire to find the male heir that his first wife, Catherine of Aragon, had not given him. When their daughter Mary came to the throne in 1553, after the death of her younger half-brother King Edward VI, she vigorously attempted to restore English loyalty to the Church of Rome. Several hundred earnest Protestants—men and women with spiritual commitments far deeper than the late King Henry's—were burnt at the stake, soon to be memorialized in *Foxe's Book of Martyrs* (1563), a landmark work that left an indelible impression on the culture of radical Protestants. Mary's repression drove other Protestants to seek safety on the continent, where some were deeply influenced by the Calvinist Reformed movement. After Mary died in 1558, her redheaded half-sister Elizabeth, daughter of the executed Anne Boleyn, came to the throne. Elizabeth returned England to Protestant rule, and the Catholic share of its population diminished with each decade. Elizabeth, too, worked hard to attain a unified church. But the Marian exiles who returned from Holland and other Reformed communities, like John Calvin's Geneva, carried more radical ideas. In their view, the Church of England needed further purification so that it would not remain a nationalized version of the Church of Rome, with its hierarchy of bishops and its overly liturgical worship.

That concern inspired the Puritan movement that played so vital a role in the shaping of American Protestantism. The next chapter will consider the religious significance of Puritanism in its American context. What matters now is the recognition that in late sixteenth- and seventeenth-century England, disputes within a predominantly Protestant nation generated the debates over religious liberty and repeated calls for toleration that formed the original background for American thinking.

Five monarchs and one quasi-king, the Lord Protector Oliver Cromwell, reigned over England during the thirteen decades from the accession of Elizabeth I in 1558 to the deposition of James II in 1688. The dominant impulse of Elizabeth and the four Stuart kings[22]—with the potentially interesting exception of James II— was to preserve the authority of the Church of England and limit the growth of rival sects. In general they pursued a policy of religious *moderation*, as that term was then used. Moderation could still mean avoiding extremes of behavior, such as tyranny or anarchy; but it also entailed the vigorous projection of the power of the state. As the historian Ethan Shagan observes, strong notions of "governance, restraint, repression and control were built into the very language of moderation, which could be a path of domination as much as a path of accommodation."[23] This attitude was perfectly consistent with the repression of the Puritan movement, particularly under the persecutions led by Archbishop William Laud in the 1620s; with the brutal suppression of Quakers and other overzealous enthusiasts after the Restoration of Stuart rule in 1660; with the adoption of the Conventicle Acts of 1664 and 1670 designed to punish dissenters for engaging in any form of worship outside the Church of England. All of these regulatory exercises conducted in the name of moderation sought to preserve a "middle way" in which the authority of the state and its established church remained paramount.

What made this policy appear so compelling was the experience of the two mid-century decades that carried the British Isles into the civil war of the 1640s and the Republican and commonwealth experiments that followed the execution of Charles I outside the Banqueting House at Whitehall palace on January 30, 1649. (John Locke's school, Westminster, was nearby.) With the suppression of the Church of England, the Presbyterian and Independent strains of the Puritan movement struggled to control the nation's religious life, Presbyterians favoring church government directed by councils of the ministry and lay elders, Independents preferring greater autonomy for individual congregations. Presbyterians enjoyed the advantage early in the civil war. But in the second phase of conflict the Independent-dominated New Model Army, led by Oliver Cromwell, came to power, leading to the execution of Charles I. Independents were more tolerant of the smaller groupings of religious dissenters that were also flourishing amid the civic chaos. These dissenting groups included the Baptists, who already had a trans-Atlantic base of operations in colonial Rhode Island, and such sects as Quakers, Seekers, Ranters, and Fifth Monarchists (all terms of opprobrium leveled by their critics).

The existence of this spiritual hothouse pulled the men and women of mid-century England in different, often confusing, and vexatious directions. The "proliferation of sects" could be read as proof that a severe divine judgment was afflicting the entire nation. Puritan clergy could view the loss of their congregants either to more radical sects or to spiritual indifference as a clarion against the toleration of diversity. Amid this turmoil countless tracts pled for religious tolerance, yet that concept retained its familiar burdensome meaning. "As a rule, toleration was a dirty word in Puritan England," Blair Worden observes. "It stood not for an edifying principle but for an impious policy."[24] A handful of religiously charged voices, notably including John Milton and Roger Williams (a genuinely Atlantic figure), endorsed broad claims for freedom of conscience in order to liberate individuals to pursue their religious destiny. But most calls for toleration were designed to protect the interests and security of one's own sect. Calvinist belief was far too dogmatic to imagine a peaceful, open competition of denominations.

The Restoration of Charles II in 1660 led to the full reestablishment of the Church of England. The new king was not committed to a policy of religious repression, and was willing to seek practical accommodations with religious dissenters. But the long Cavalier Parliament (1661–1678) had other intentions. Not only was it reluctant to yield full legal authority over the regulation of religious matters to the royal prerogative. It was also intent on enabling the Church of England to again become a truly national church. Many members of Parliament vainly hoped that the dissenters would abandon their beliefs and practices. These wayward enthusiasts should reckon with the national turmoil their dissent had sparked and restore England's identity as a unified Protestant kingdom.

To pursue these objectives, Parliament enacted two kinds of measures, penal laws and Test Acts. The penal laws sought to limit unlicensed religious gatherings taking place outside the Church of England by subjecting violators to special taxes, costly penalties, and imprisonment. Within the walls of one's home, in the sanctity of one's conscience, families and individuals might still worship as they wished. In that sense the Conventicle Acts tacitly recognized a zone of privacy below the regulatory authority of the state.[25] But that minimal definition hardly allowed sectarians to express their religious views freely in either a communal or public setting. In a celebrated trial that was also a milestone in the history of the jury, William Penn and William Mead were tried at the Old Bailey on September 1, 1670, charged with disturbing the peace simply for preaching Quaker doctrine outside their meetinghouse on the eponymous Gracechurch Street in east London.[26] The Test Acts of 1673 and 1678 had a different objective. Their purpose was to require Roman Catholic recusants to renounce core doctrines of their church, such as transubstantiation and papal supremacy, and also to deny public office to those holding dissenting or Catholic beliefs.[27]

None of these harsh procedures tempered the ardor of radical Protestants. Once released, the genie of conscience and the desire to lead a religious life consistent with one's moral commitments could not be restrained. Quakers and Baptists could not be tamed, and if Presbyterians and Independents yielded their old ambitions for ecclesiastical reform, they still opposed the practices and hierarchy of the Church of England.

The restrictions that Parliament imposed embodied policies that Charles II and James II sought to relax. They would have used their prerogative of indulgence—that is, their authority to refuse to enforce particular laws—to relieve the grievances of radical

Dissenters and Catholics alike. Part of this policy rested on the monarchs' Catholic sympathies. In negotiating the French alliance sealed in the Treaty of Dover (1670), Charles II secretly pledged his eventual conversion to the Church of Rome. James was a Catholic all along, and deeply attached to the devotional practices of "avant-garde French catholicism."[28] Yet both brothers also understood that a monarchical commitment to toleration for both Dissenters and Catholics might strengthen their rule by diluting the most potent source of civic tension within English society.

Charles's efforts to use indulgences to advance toleration were thwarted by the militant opposition of Parliament and the Church. Many factors account for this failure: bitter memories of the civil war and the martyrdom of Charles I; disgust with the ongoing outrageous behavior of Dissenters, especially the Quakers who merrily violated every norm they disdained; and fears of "popery," which meant not only distaste for Catholic beliefs and practices but the conviction that Catholics owed political allegiance to a foreign potentate. Moreover, any effort to use the prerogative of indulgence inevitably raised the same basic questions about the balance of royal and parliamentary powers that had sparked the recurring constitutional disputes of the seventeenth century.

The most ambitious attempt to further the cause of toleration came, however, from James II, near the end of his brief kingship. Many assessments of this campaign depend on how one views its relation to the Glorious Revolution of 1688, yet another vexed subject.[29] But his effort to repeal the penal laws offers a valuable commentary on the problem of religious toleration at the close of the century.

As Duke of York, James treated religious toleration as a grant of a legal privilege that worthy individuals could claim and unworthy ones forfeit. He opposed the use of force and legal prosecutions over matters of religion but did not yet regard "liberty of conscience as an indefeasible natural right."[30] Once James came to the throne in 1685, however, he developed a more ambitious agenda. Because of his friendship and alliance with William Penn, the earliest beneficiaries of the king's new policy included Quakers as well as Catholics.[31] The decisive moment came in April 1687, when the king issued a *Declaration for Liberty of Conscience* safeguarding the worship of Catholics and dissenters, and then ordered its public reading by the Church of England. The publication of this indulgence produced a sharp reaction from the Anglican clergy. But after the king dissolved his first Parliament and issued a new call for elections, the supporters of his indulgence, who were sometimes labeled "repealers" of the onerous statutes, formed an active movement aimed at giving James a pliable majority in the House of Commons. In effect, James was promoting a referendum on his policy. With vigorous assistance from Penn, the king effectively campaigned in behalf of his measure. And he did all this on the explicit ground of providing a new Magna Carta of religious liberty. As the king told a group of Whig gentlemen in the town of Chester, he "hoped we would join with him in making a magna Charta for conscience as well as properties and other liberties." In Penn's view, such an act would make toleration a fundamental right, in effect giving it constitutional status (within the English meaning of that term).[32]

If taken at face value these were noble sentiments, and at the start of the king's campaign they elicited many positive responses, from both his Catholic supporters and Dissenters.[33] Some observers agreed that the benefits of a policy of toleration outweighed constitutional qualms as to whether a royal indulgence was the best vehicle for relief. But however one assesses James's idea of a Magna Carta of conscience, the other planks of his monarchist program doomed his campaign to failure. If one follows the recent influential work of Steven Pincus on the Glorious Revolution, James intended to rule as an advocate of Catholic modernity in the French (or Gallican) style.

"From the moment of his accession," Pincus observes, James sought to do "everything he could to create a modern, rational, centralized Catholic state," along the lines modeled by Louis XIV.[34] The efforts that James made to catholicize the Church of England ultimately persuaded Dissenters to move into opposition. The decisive test came in the spring of 1688, after James issued a second indulgence that Anglican clergy were ordered to read from their pulpits. The defiance of this request by seven Anglican bishops led to their trial for seditious libel against the king, a charge that generated immense public outrage in their favor and ended with their triumphal acquittal by a London jury on June 29, 1688. Only partly coincidentally, on the next day William of Orange received the invitation of the seven Whig leaders seeking his active militant intervention in English affairs with the implicit invitation to displace the sitting king.[35]

However one assesses James's intentions, whether one sees him as a potentially enlightened architect of a religious Magna Carta or an artful absolutist seeking to co-opt his political opposition, his bid for religious toleration could never outweigh his Catholic and Francophile commitments. These were the dominant political facts of his brief reign, compounded by the birth of a male heir three weeks before the trial of the seven bishops. No amount of active campaigning could ease the suspicions of his motives. In the wake of the revocation of the Edict of Nantes, no Whig constitutionalist could trust a proto-absolutist monarch who stoutly valued his prerogative to issue indulgences or suspend parliamentary statutes. That notion of prerogative defied the understanding of supreme parliamentary authority embedded in the Declaration of Rights that William and Mary had to accept as a condition of their ascension to the throne.

The culmination of these events was the passage of the Act of Toleration by the new Parliament. Whether that is the best title for this act is a matter of scholarly dispute. Its true title is "An act to exempt their Majesties' Protestant subjects dissenting from the Church of England from the penalties of certain laws" that had not been repealed.[36] The act did not apply to Catholics. Individuals who refused to take their sacraments within the Church of England could neither attend Oxford and Cambridge colleges nor serve in Parliament. Non-Trinitarians were still liable to charges of heresy; English's two greatest minds, the new friends Isaac Newton and John Locke, knew they had to keep their Socinian leanings utterly private.[37] Other parts of the act were the result of intense political maneuverings. Some Tory members of Parliament wanted the act to have a seven-year sunset clause. An attempt to accompany the Act of Toleration with an act of comprehension that would have enabled Dissenters to reenter the Church of England failed of passage. All in all, this remained a very *politique* measure in the French use of that term. It was not a broad statement of natural rights or libertarian principles, but rather a negotiated effort to produce a decent measure of civic peace. If it limited the scope of royal prerogative, it did not diminish the authority of Parliament over religious affairs.[38] Just as a Stuart king remained free to evoke his gracious indulgence, so Parliament retained full legislative authority to expand its regulation of religion, if it so wished.

## LOCKE'S CONCEPT OF TOLERATION

The seventeenth-century English controversy over the restoration of religious uniformity and the offsetting appeals for the free exercise of conscience produced a vast archive of tracts and treatises. Numerous pamphlets were written as ongoing polemical exchanges between writers, whose identities are sometimes known but often left anonymous. The most famous of these works is John Locke's *Letter Concerning Toleration*, published shortly after he returned to

England from his Dutch exile. In many respects, Locke's *Letter* was a postscript to a debate that had largely run its course, restating arguments other writers had already made familiar. Had the *Letter* appeared before Parliament adopted its Act of Toleration, it might have gained some measure of immediate political influence. Instead Locke found himself embroiled in a long-running controversy with Jonas Proast, a Tory High-Church Anglican, which led him to write two further *Letters* and draft a third reply that only his staunchest students now read.[39]

Yet Locke's initial *Letter*, which he drafted in 1685 while the revocation of Edict of Nantes was being implemented, remains a morally compelling statement of religious toleration. It is arguably the one text that serves as the best base line for tracing the emerging American commitment to the free exercise of religion. Equally important, the biographical dimensions of Locke's positions illustrate how his own life reflected the process of individual religious choice that he wished to defend. To understand Locke's relation to American thinking, it is helpful to situate his *Letter* in its proper context, and to appreciate both its achievements and its perceived limitations.

Locke (1632–1704) was baptized in the Church of England but came from a family with Calvinist and Presbyterian leanings. He was an older student at Westminster School, which retained a strongly Anglican cast. As first a student and then a don at Christ Church College, Oxford, Locke joined a strongly Calvinist institution. Yet at some early point, his familial ties to Calvinist convictions lapsed.[40] Locke always worshipped within the Church of England, but his theology, his search for religious truth, remained an active, dynamic, and essential element of his thinking and morality throughout his life.[41] Locke found it difficult, indeed impossible to imagine a moral system that did not depend on a belief in divine reward and punishment in a world to come. He is regarded, rather anachronistically, as the founder of modern liberalism, but one cannot understand his thinking without coming to grips with his deep religious commitments.

Locke's thoughts on religious toleration were also dynamic. Yet here the key changes occurred at an early age. The Christ Church student and tutor of the early 1660s welcomed the Restoration of Charles II and the full legal reestablishment of the Church of England as healthy measures. He viewed the two decades of civil war and Interregnum as a chaotic travail that the royal government would do well to reverse. On one critical point that had long roiled English politics, he defended the capacity of the government to regulate "indifferent" matters—that is, religious practices that "were not commanded by God either through natural law or Revelation." For nonconformist dissenters, enjoying the leeway to ignore or avoid *adiaphora* was a hallmark of what toleration would mean. Firmly sympathetic with the Anglican cause of religious retrenchment, the young Locke disputed this view. In two unpublished manuscripts now known as *Two Tracts on Government*, Locke faulted dissenting preachers for unleashing the contentious voices of their adherents. It was well within the authority of government, he argued, to regulate such practices in the name of social peace and personal civility, and well within the duty of subjects to adhere to such lawful decisions.[42]

Five years later, however, in another unpublished "Essay on Toleration," Locke altered his views. The reasons for this change remain obscure, but its substance does not. By the late 1660s, Locke was growing more skeptical of the techniques being used by the Church of England to enforce conformity, and more sensitive to the value of allowing individuals to indulge their own ideas about ritual as a means for attaining or maintaining true faith. The key shift is that Locke grew more inclined to err on the side of toleration rather than emphasize the putative advantages of conformity.[43] Locke also actively considered, as a serious question, whether toleration could be applied to Catholics.[44]

Over the roughly two decades that separated the drafting of the "Essay on Toleration" from the writing and publication of his *Letter Concerning Toleration*, these views developed richly. That period brought the continued harassment and persecution of numerous dissenters, including the Quaker enthusiasts who languished and perished by the thousands in English jails. It saw the increased severity of the French monarchy's campaign against the Huguenots, which Locke monitored from Holland. And there, too, Locke gathered fresh evidence of the way in which a regime of toleration could actually work.[45] If the Revocation inspired the drafting of the *Letter Concerning Toleration*, events in England provided additional evidence of its continued relevance. Many of the "repealers" who supported the two indulgences granted by James II still hoped for the best outcome, but Locke counted himself among those who viewed the king's initiatives as a catholicizing, absolutist plot that Britons were bound to resist.

Locke's *Letter* restated and synthesized ideas made familiar from previous decades of debate. To take one noteworthy example, William Walwyn, in his 1645 tract *A Helpe to the right understanding of a Discourse Concerning Independency*, offered a broad defense of religious conscience not only as an "inalienable possession" of individuals but as a prototype for "a whole range of powers and rights that could not be surrendered to the state without violating God's orders."[46] Yet Locke did present his main positions with a striking clarity, and without immersing himself in the specific contours of English (or British) history. Thus although it would be a grave historical error to make Locke the decisive or most influential figure in the development of religious toleration, it remains enormously helpful to allow his arguments to serve as an intellectual focal point for later commentators. (On the American side, one can make the same claim for Jefferson and Madison.)

Locke's first argument—the one with the greatest constitutional significance—rested on a clear delineation of the respective spheres of church and state. Here Locke argued quite directly that it is "above all things necessary to distinguish exactly the Business of Civil Government from that of Religion." The former involved the creation of a "Commonwealth" by a "Society of Men constituted only for the procuring, preserving, and securing of their own *Civil Interests*," which comprehended "Life, Liberty, Health, and Indolency of Body, and the Possession of outward things, such as Money, Lands, Houses, Furniture, and the like." Such a commonwealth "hath nothing to do with the World to come." A church has a wholly different character. It is simply "a voluntary Society of Men, joining themselves together of their own accord, in order to the publick worshipping of God, in such a manner as they judge acceptable to him, and effectual to the salvation of their Souls." Over such "a free and voluntary Society," the state has no authority—and certainly no power to coerce belief.[47]

It lacks that authority, in the second place, because the state has no greater capacity than the morally sovereign individual to decide what form of worship is most suitable to salvation. Christianity depends on interior belief, and belief and faith can never be coerced. The God who created us wishes individuals to worship him in the way that is most consistent with our own convictions. This is a duty that we independently owe to God, and which in certain respects precedes our responsibilities to the state. A hollow conformity to outward norms that are legally imposed sacrifices the sincerity that God desires; it is simply a form of hypocrisy. These arguments have a fundamentally Christian, even Protestant character: they focus, first and foremost, on matters of faith defined as interior convictions. Yet Locke (in some ways echoing Montaigne) also reminds readers that "every Prince is Orthodox to himself," and that Christians would therefore be entirely vulnerable to persecution in other societies if one conceded the authority of the state to regulate religious belief and worship.

The state does, however, retain the capacity to restrict or prohibit the behavior of several categories of individuals. In certain respects, Locke retained a *politique* attitude toward protecting the security of civil society. In his famous exceptions, toleration need not be extended to Catholics, atheists, or those who deny toleration to others. The former cannot be trusted because they owe their loyalty to a foreign prince—the pope, who has already instructed his adherents that they need not honor their obligations to heretics. Atheists suffer a similar debility. Lacking belief in divine judgment in the world to come, they, too, will act irresponsibly in this world whenever they can get away with it. Here again Locke's political and civic morality remained firmly embedded in the necessity of religious belief. "The taking away of God, though but even in thought, dissolves all."

To many modern observers, then, Locke seems a less advanced thinker than we want him to be. In matters of toleration, his two notable contemporaries, Spinoza and Bayle, went admirably further.[48] They were prepared to be more tolerant of the rights of Catholics and atheists, more inclined to make overt acts rather than cautionary premonitions the basis of judging these doubtful groups. Yet critical judgments such as these transgress the historians' basic duty to avoid anachronism; they turn a complicated problem of historical explanation into a restatement of Whig history. The problem is not to understand or evaluate the sources of Locke's limitations— if such they were—but to explain why he found them so compelling. Locke's immediate concern, as John Dunn argues, was to justify the freedom to worship on latitudinarian, comprehensive grounds, not to fashion a general theory of the freedom of thought or expression.[49] Within a Protestant world reacting against the abuses of the

Revocation or the specter of a Catholic absolutist monarchy, his position remained entirely sensible.

There are nevertheless three important reasons why Locke's approach to religious toleration remains highly relevant to the multidenominational American situation.

First, Locke's definitional effort to distinguish the proper concerns of civil government from the free and voluntary nature of religious association did mark an important step toward the idea of the separation of state and church. Locke could not complete that notion of separation, because prudential concerns, especially those relating to Catholic loyalties, justified a residual power to monitor religious activities. But remove the threats that still troubled Locke, and the road to separation would lie open.

Second, although Locke's conception of the freedom of conscience from coercion was not novel, his emphasis on conscience as the defining characteristic of religious identity did embrace the idea of a morally sovereign individual, exercising a fundamental right no authority could deny. Because Locke was personally indifferent (in the modern sense) to the ritualized performance of "indifferent things" (in their historical meaning), he treated men and women as autonomous beings who had a duty to worship god as each saw fit. This was a natural right in the full sense of the term, because it depended on the idea that religious belief was finally a matter of inward persuasion and conviction that could never be coerced. Locke wanted to secure the free exercise of religion as a means to a greater end, and that end had a deeply egalitarian and liberal quality.

Third, as an extension of this point, Locke recognized that individual autonomy had a pronounced generational aspect. This aspect of his thinking has not received the attention it merits. Locke opened his discussion of the "free and voluntary" character of a church by declaring that "No body is born a Member of any Church. Otherwise the Religion of Parents would descend unto Children, by the same right of Inheritance as their Temporal Estates, and every one would hold his Faith by the same Tenure he does his Lands; than which nothing can be imagined more absurd."[50] In any contest between the family and the state over the religious instruction of children, Locke would have doubtless sided with the rights of the father and mother. He knew what the French monarchy had been doing with Huguenot children, and he could never approve that cruel assertion of the authority of the state. Yet just as rulers were trustees for their commonwealths, so parents were trustees for their children, not owners. Children could be reared in the traditions of their families, but they were ultimately entitled to their own choice—the kind of choice Locke had exercised in moving away from the dominant religious commitments of his family.

These conditions had deep relevance to the development of religious life in colonial America, making Locke a relevant authority for understanding the emergence of a distinctive approach to the rights of conscience and the free exercise of religion. If it is indeed helpful or even essential to have philosophically compelling statements of the general principles of religious toleration or free exercise as a point of departure, Locke is as good a place to begin as any. Struggling with the modest limitations of his ideas also allows thoughtful readers to glimpse their more ambitious possibilities.

## CHAPTER TWO

# The Liberty of Conscience and Conversion

WHEN JOHN LOCKE deemed it "absurd" to imagine that children inherited their parents' religious convictions in the same way as they inherited property, he tacitly invoked his own biography and theology. Of course, in religion as in politics, inherited loyalties matter a lot, and many enthusiastic sects soon acquire a tribal character that they wish to pass from generation to generation. But the kinds of religious commitments that affected many American colonists proved especially intense because they required individuals to make conscious choices about their ideas of salvation. These commitments pivoted either on experiencing a religious conversion or, alternatively, on aligning with denominations that emphasized an individual's voluntary and rational capacity to acquire saving faith. The publicly professed experience of conversion played a key role in the formation of the Calvinist churches of seventeenth-century New England. The two great religious revivals of the mid-eighteenth and early nineteenth centuries, the First and Second Great Awakenings, replicated that emphasis. The colonists increasingly viewed the exercise of religious conscience as a natural right that belonged equally to men and women.

One cannot understand the evolution of a distinctly American conception of free exercise until one takes these aspects of religiosity into account. The single most important fact of colonial religious life was the existence in New England of a radical experiment that quickly focused on the direct experience of conversion tied to the psychologically unsettling demands of predestination. In England the Independent and Presbyterian movements with whom American Puritans were aligned had flourished during the mid-century decades of the 1640s and 1650s but thereafter struggled as dissenting sects resisting Restoration repression. But their Puritan counterparts abroad gained a prolonged opportunity to create godly commonwealths in Congregational Massachusetts, Presbyterian Connecticut, and Baptist Rhode Island. The complicated narratives of their efforts dominate the religious history of the colonial era, with lasting consequences for the evolution of American ideas of religious freedom.[1]

A principled belief in religious freedom as a right to be extended to all was *not* a value that the colonists gladly packed in the cultural baggage they carried from Britain. The majority of Puritans in the Great Migration of 1630–1642 were orthodox Calvinists who were perfectly content to persecute their more radical brethren. The Antinomians (like Anne Hutchinson), Baptists (like Roger Williams), and Quakers (like William Penn) whom they distrusted, detested, and sometimes persecuted were equally candid in repudiating the tenets of other denominations. Rhode Island and Pennsylvania became sites of disestablishment, but the radical dissenters they protected harbored their own enthusiasms and dislikes. There, too, individuals expressed their religious beliefs in the biting tongue of acrimony and anathema. The Church of England, which was legally established in other colonies, also retained its ingrained intolerance of dissenters.

At first glance, then, the bare fact that the colonies became an attractive refuge for religious dissenters did not guarantee that toleration and free expression would evolve into legal rights that Americans broadly accepted. Yet that development did occur, not because the colonists had sudden intellectual revelations of the value of this principle, but as the consequence of an array of factors. In crucial respects, the acceptance of this principle was a byproduct of the substantive content of religious beliefs. And foremost among these (I want to propose) was the enormous importance that individual decisions about conversion played in the lives of ordinary Protestants. That concern made the protection of conscience and free expression fundamental rights, in a situation where the authority of established religion was much weaker than it was in Europe.

The colonists who settled British North America occupied a spiritual landscape that bore no resemblance to the Old World. There was, of course, a sacred landscape that the continent's aboriginal inhabitants already inhabited, full of landmarks replete with spiritual meanings. But that was a landscape that few colonists ever glimpsed or tried to comprehend. Most colonists dismissed Native American religious practices as the work of heathens and devil worshippers, peoples practicing "the grossest ignorance, delusions, and most stupid paganism," as the influential eighteenth-century minister Jonathan Edwards complained. Individual colonists who lived in close proximity to native communities and therefore learned something about their spiritual beliefs and practices could reject these crude attitudes. But such sympathizers were few and far between.[2]

It took some generations for the colonists to "sacralize" this landscape. Save for the spare meetinghouses where New England Puritans listened to sermons and pondered the puzzle of predestination, seventeenth-century America had few churches. "Without explicitly rejecting traditional English patterns," the historian Jon Butler observes, seventeenth-century Virginians "were shaping an American landscape remarkably free of the church buildings that overflowed the humanly shaped environment at home." Only toward the turn of the eighteenth century, when the initial colonizing phase of British settlement gave way to the provincial period that followed, did serious efforts begin to construct sturdy places of worship.[3] But most of these churches were modest in size and plainly decorated.

There were other obvious ways in which European and American landscapes diverged. Outside New England, much of the colonial population scattered across the countryside, living on farms and plantations that were isolated from each other. In New England, with its tightly settled nuclear villages of forty or fifty families surrounded by outlying fields and pastures, the idea of a community acting as a *corpus Christianum* still held. One leading historian of early New England has aptly described these villages as Closed Christian Corporate Utopian Communities.[4] But applying that term to the scattered plantations of Virginia or the Carolinas would make little sense.

More important, the virtual absence of Catholics from British North America stripped the spiritual landscape of the symbols, practices, and habits that drove European Protestants into militant action. There were no altars to strip, or statues or ornate windows to smash, or public processions of the Host to scoff; no monasteries or nunneries to tear down; no saints' days to violate. Nor were there any disciplined Jesuit priests milling around to stir faithful Catholic crowds to harass Protestant churches and processions. Even Maryland, founded as a Catholic refuge under the proprietorship of the Calvert family, soon became a Protestant society. In the few communities where they settled, Catholics were content simply to worship privately, without all the public performance of religiosity that was so conspicuous in Europe. In a sense, they had to become quietists. Protestants retained their traditional animosity against the Church of Rome, but there was no visible Catholic presence they needed to oppose or repress. The real Catholic enemy lived north of the St. Lawrence River, in Quebec—an external threat to colonial security rather than an internal danger to the community. Colonial Protestants remained free to expend their energies reading Scripture and earnestly contesting countless doctrinal points. But they escaped many of the sources of religious conflict and persecution that operated as flashpoints (to repeat Benjamin Kaplan's term) for open conflict in Europe.

The cultural differences between the performance of religion in Europe and in America were staggering, as David Hall's important book, *Worlds of Wonder, Days of Judgment*, nicely captures. Building on a famous passage of Henry James contrasting the situations of European and American novelists ("no palaces, no castles, nor manors"), as personified in the work of Nathaniel Hawthorne, Hall similarly invokes the absence of so many symbols from the daily religious life that historians strive to reconstruct:

> No cathedrals, nor abbeys, nor little Norman churches [as James had also written]; no liturgy, as in the Book of Common Prayer; no tithes to pay the clergy, no ranks of bishop and archbishop, no church courts nor processions of the clergy; no altars or candles, no prayers for the dead.
>
> And let us move beyond the narrowly religious:
>
> No saints days or Christmas, no weddings or church ales, no pilgrimages, nor sacred places, nor relics or ex-votos; no "churching" after childbirth, no godparents or maypoles, no fairy tales, no dancing on the Sabbath, no carnival![5]

In this world the physical, visible, public performance of religion was far more modest. Protestant spirituality was devoted to interior conviction rather than outward observance.

Yet societies dominated by radical Protestants were fully capable of generating prolonged and bitter doctrinal disputes. That was especially the case in New England. The animating principle of Puritan religious life was the sermon, delivered by a minister who had been *called* to a particular congregation, just as the concept of *calling* described other facets of life. It was the quality of the sermon, more than the trappings of the church, which Puritans prized; and it was the contents of this preaching that shaped the religious challenges that their communities faced.

The settlement of colonial New England forms one of the most closely studied subjects in early American history—or American history more generally. Many of the outlines of this field were set by three of the nation's most eminent historians: Perry Miller, the great student of *The New England Mind*, and two scholars who studied with him, Edmund S. Morgan and Bernard Bailyn, who became dominant figures at Yale and Harvard. Together they trained scores of students who have written an equivalent number of learned volumes on a wide array of topics, from, say, the demographic history of the first *Four Generations* of Andover, Massachusetts to *The Logic of Millennial Thought*.[6] And, of course, squads, platoons, and whole companies of scholars trained at other institutions have also contributed to this vastly researched field.

Yet the one book that arguably matters most for our purposes is a slender set of lectures that Edmund Morgan originally gave at New York University in 1962. *Visible Saints: The History of a Puritan Idea*[7] is a historian's detective story that focuses on a particular problem. At what point, and for what purposes, did the first generation of Puritans create the defining practice of the New England Way: the decision to make persuasive public testimony of one's experience of conversion the basis for gaining full membership in the local church, and with it the right to take communion and have one's children receive the sacraments of baptism and communion? That decision worked quite well for the twice-winnowed members of the founding generation, the men and women who freely joined the Puritan movement in England and the Great Migration to America. They had ample reason to believe that they were fulfilling a providential purpose and that God had twice singled them out to advance this "Errand into the Wilderness" (the title of one of Miller's interesting essays).

Their second- and third-generation children and grandchildren, however, had very different experiences. Though they remained theologically orthodox, they did not come forward in large numbers to testify to their conversions. Growing up the descendants of "visible saints," they may have found it spiritually or psychologically impossible to replicate the experience of their formidable ancestors. Their reticence posed a troubling challenge, for at some point, the basis for maintaining full membership in individual churches would be endangered. The Halfway Covenant proposed by a ministerial synod in 1662 offered one partial answer to this problem. The grandchildren of the original members could be baptized, in the hope that they would grow up to own the covenant in all its details. But many churches delayed endorsing and implementing this compromise, clinging to the original practices of the 1630s.

Morgan's story pivots on a crucial shift in the Puritans' understanding of the process and purpose of conversion. Predestination, when taken literally as Calvinists were bound to take it, is a terrifying idea. It restores to God the total sovereignty that the Church of Rome had diluted with its reliance on good works and repentance as paths to salvation. In the Puritan regime, parents and their maturing children must struggle to gain the saving faith that all Christians want to profess, yet not grow too confident of the evidence they uncover (see Proverbs 16: 18). Periods of doubt are likely to intervene, as individuals measure the puzzles of the doctrine against the failings of their lives and souls and their interior doubts. In the worst case, the anxiety this quest provokes gives rise to suicidal tendencies out of a simple desire to end the suspense and learn the true answer.

English Puritan ministers had to wrestle with the anxieties this doctrine evoked in their adherents. Without denying God's ultimate unknowable sovereignty over salvation, they developed a method that would enable the laity (and perhaps the ministry, too) to maintain their belief in salvation by faith alone. In Morgan's account, these ministers identified a set of stages that earnest believers had to complete to acquire a reasonable if necessarily imperfect conviction of their likelihood of salvation. Morgan uses the phrase "morphology of conversion" to describe this spiritual awakening; to a modern reader they sound much like a twelve-stage process to overcome a crippling addiction. In England this process was meant to spur religious faith and had no relation to one's membership in the visible church of a worldly congregation. But in New England the test of saving faith acquired a radically new purpose: to provide a workable formula for creating churches modeled on the primitive congregations that preceded the formation of the Church of Rome.[8] The full members of a properly formed church would then consist of mature individuals who could render convincing testimony of their conversion. A congregation would begin to form with the public testimony of a few select individuals, and then the circle would widen as other neighbors made their own account. There is no smoking pulpit in Morgan's detective story, but the influential preaching of John Cotton played a prominent role in the emergence of the New England system.[9]

This decision, which conformed so well to the experience of the first generation immigrants, set New England Puritanism on its unique path. It also sparked two sources of tension—one generational, the other denominational—that reverberated through the Puritan movement and early American Protestantism more generally. The failure of the second and third generations to own the covenant challenged the success of the Puritan experiment. Eventually, after late seventeenth-century New England suffered other setbacks, congregations did accept the moderating impulses of the Halfway Covenant.[10] Moreover, instead of making baptism and communion the *reward* of full membership, Puritan ministers began to regard these two sacraments as *incentives* for spiritual growth. Early eighteenth-century Puritanism had lost the radical edge of the founding generation—until the great revival that began circa 1735–1740 restored the Calvinist vigor that had prevailed a century earlier and again made the professed experience of conversion the spiritual goal of awakened Protestants.

This cycle of belief can still be seen in the terms in which Edmund Morgan once described it. Too great a zeal for spiritual purity must eventually end in a moderation or relaxation of religious practices, but this in turn will ultimately spark calls for a revival of the original, stricter standards. For our purposes, however, the crucial fact is to recognize the enormous importance that Puritan orthodoxy placed on encouraging every individual, in each generation, to search inwardly, to monitor his or her soul for signs of saving faith, and to anticipate the prospect of conversion, even if it never came. American Calvinists occupied a religious world where the demands of conscience never ceased, where men and women had to balance a fluid ledger of beliefs and doubts, complicated by their own idiosyncratic interpretations of Scripture. In this society, no one could afford to abandon the exercise of conscience. The force of this demand varied over time, from generation to generation, but it never disappeared from religious culture, and it periodically resurged with amazing force.

Arguably the strongest resurgence came with the Great Awakening, which was precipitated in part by the writings of Jonathan Edwards (1703–1758) and the itinerant preaching of

George Whitefield (1714–1770), a younger founder of English Methodism. Edwards was eighteenth-century America's preeminent theologian, and the cross-eyed Whitefield the most commanding preacher of his age. Together, their writings and sermons revived the importance that seventeenth-century Puritans had placed on conversion and renewed the idea that only the converted could form the nucleus of a properly constituted church. Equally important, the dramatic impact of revivalism split several denominations in two, creating New and Old Light Congregationalists and New and Old Side Presbyterians. This contributed to the shattering of denominational unity that in turn laid the foundation for the flourishing spiritual marketplace—that great nexus of religious competition—that permeated post-Revolutionary America.

## SOURCES OF DENOMINATIONAL DIVERSITY

Down to the mid-eighteenth century, the ministers who led the Puritan movement worked hard to maintain doctrinal orthodoxy. With their training at Cambridge University or Harvard College in that other Cambridge on the Charles River, and later at Yale College, this corps of well-educated ministers understood the importance of their preaching. Predestination is not only a terrifying doctrine to accept but also a difficult doctrine to comprehend, and Puritan ministers repeatedly had to explain to their congregants how to reconcile a divine decision that no one could alter with a believer's obligation to receive grace and pursue saving faith.

Yet convictions and conditions made orthodoxy impossible to preserve. From the outset, the Puritan movement sprouted its own radical fruit. The civil government of Massachusetts wanted to maintain a religiously homogeneous commonwealth, but the Great Migration included a number of radically experimental individuals, some of whom left England to escape the increasingly repressive policies of Archbishop Laud. "By the 1640s," Philip Gura observes,

> New England Congregationalists (as well as their conservative English critics) complained that the colonies harbored self deluded (or merely disguised) spiritualists, antinomians, familists, Seekers, Anabaptists, Ranters, Adamites, and Quakers, all implicitly aligned against the established church system because of their insistence that an individual's personal religious experience supercede the demands of ecclesiastical tradition and civil law.[11]

Not all of these terms need definition here, but three merit brief explanation. Antinomians held that God communicated with them directly, conveying a true knowledge of their saving faith that liberated them from ordinary obedience to law. Anabaptists (or simply Baptists) carried Puritan doctrine to a logical but deeply disturbing conclusion: If conversion was the essential prerequisite for admission to the sacraments, then baptism should be done not at childbirth, but only after one had enjoyed (or suffered) the requisite spiritual experience. Baptists felt little need for an educated ministry, trained to unsort theological complexities. Spirited lay preachers, itinerants on the land, were all they required. Quakers also felt no need for ministers of any kind, or for sermons. Later generations of the Society of Friends acquired a reputation for moral earnestness and sobriety. One simply attended a meetinghouse whose members faced each other, waiting for the Inward Light—the divine voice— to spur one to testimony. But the sect's founding members were a rowdy, enthusiastic, and obnoxious crew. As Teresa Bejan observes, "Quakers were notorious for going naked in public 'for a sign,' as well as interrupting others' worship by banging pots and pans or shouting down the minister."[12]

Indeed, Quaker behavior was so offensive that even Roger Williams, the effective founder of Rhode Island, held them in open contempt. In popular thinking, Williams is often regarded as the one advocate of broad toleration whose concerns were primarily religious in nature—the one who recognized that we should individually bestow equal respect on everyone who is actively searching for the form of worship that best accords with his or her individual notion of what God wants from us. Yet Williams retained the fierce Calvinist convictions he acquired as a boy, and he acidly dismissed many of the religious views he encountered, even in Puritan Massachusetts, from which he was eventually banished. The form of toleration that Williams favored, Bejan argues in her brilliant book, was a "mere civility" that would provide a *minimal* level of social peace rather than a principled acceptance of every person's right to moral autonomy. Religious views that he found erroneous remained subject to open disparagement. His formula for "mere civility" was thus an exercise in tolerance in the traditional sense: it involved finding ways to accommodate views that were theologically objectionable and morally burdensome. His approach ensured that religious disagreements would persist, but it also presumed that civil mechanisms could be found to make these discussions acceptable. The problem with Quakers was that they pushed this grudging toleration to its very limits, and then beyond. Their behavior, at least initially, fell below the minimal level of civility that Williams required. One could argue, only half perversely, that the real test of toleration in seventeenth-century America, as in England, was whether one could allow Quakers in one's community, or not.[13] Quakers came to America "bringing their lurid brand of sacred theater with them," Susan Juster observes. Not surprisingly, "the vast majority of the blasphemy records in colonial courts involved Quakers."[14]

One could make a similarly skeptical argument about the benefits of the ethnic diversity that was already beginning to flourish in the middle colonies of New York, the Jerseys, Pennsylvania, and Delaware. The history of New Netherland is often cited as a pioneering experiment in social and religious diversity and a New World extension of the toleration that already existed in the Dutch republic. From the start, many scholars have argued, the settlement that eventually became New York had a religiously diverse popula- tion who had to work out modes of toleration and accommodation to remain a viable enterprise. Dutch practices of tolerance at home thus provided helpful precedents that set the later English colony on its road to enlightenment.

In fact, as Evan Haefeli has demonstrated in a closely argued book, there was no simple model of toleration at work in Holland, nor did New York's early diversity account for the emergence of mutual patterns of religious acceptance. Dutch practice in New Netherland under the West India Company more closely resembled "the constrained pluralism of Zeeland," where Calvinists ruled with their usual discipline, than "the liberal diversity of Amsterdam," that cosmopolitan, commercial capital of toleration.[15] Even there, the Reformed Church operated as a "public church" that could conduct its worship freely, while outside groups—Catholics, Jews, and Lutherans—had to perform their services privately, out of sight (as in the *schuilkerken*). The Dutch Reformed congregations of New Netherland were not happy bearers of liberal views. The critical movement toward toleration within the province came, Haefeli argues, only after the English conquest of 1664 led to the creation of the proprietary (later royal) colony of New York and the settlement of East and West Jersey and Pennsylvania, which drew thousands of zealous Quaker to the middle colonies. The Toleration Act of 1689, with all its limitations, provided further support for a new pattern of religious acceptance, one that led to the legal establishment of the Church of England in New York and a broad recognition of the rights of dissenters.

The most radical step toward the creation of a consciously tolerant society in America came with the organization of Pennsylvania in
the early 1680s. Its proprietary founder, William Penn, qualifies as a
genuine "lawgiver" just as the political theory of the Enlightenment
defined that term: a supremely rational individual endowed with
the intellectual and moral capacity to conceive a code of laws for
the governance of an entire society. Penn's aspirations and motives
as the founding lawgiver of Pennsylvania were complex. He was
interested, first and foremost, with providing a sanctuary for his fellow Quakers, to free them from the cruel persecutions they were
receiving in Britain. He justified that position with a broad defense
of the rights of conscience that resembled Locke's *Letter Concerning
Toleration*. Penn also shared many of the constitutional views of the
Whig party that emerged during the Exclusion Crisis of 1678–1681,
when three successive Parliaments tried and failed to prevent James,
Duke of York, from being able to succeed his brother, Charles II. He
strongly supported the two cardinal axioms of Whig constitutionalism: the right to government by consent, as manifested through
political representation; and the right to trial by jury, which Penn
had purposefully supported during his own prosecution in 1670. Yet
Penn obviously enjoyed good connections with the Stuart throne,
and he actively supported James II's campaign to establish a Magna
Carta for religious liberty. Equally important, Penn understood that
economic opportunity was an essential mechanism for recruiting
population. His appeal to continental religious groups, especially
German Lutherans, thus juxtaposed giving immigrants ready access
to land with the promise of liberty of conscience.

Liberty of conscience ranked first on Penn's list of the
*Fundamental Constitutions* of the colony. Every resident of the colony
should enjoy "the free possession of his or her faith and exercise
of worship towards God, in such manner as every person shall in
conscience believe is most acceptable to God." But this definition

was constrained in another way. Drawing upon a familiar coupling in English thinking, "Christian liberty" excluded acts of "licentiousness (that is to say, to speak loosely and profanely of God, Christ, or religion, or to commit any evil in their conversation)." This last evil likely covered any verbal exchange in which one person mocked the religious beliefs of others. Anyone who would "abuse or deride any other for his or her different persuasion and practice in matters of religion shall be punished as a disturber of the peace and be punished accordingly." When John Locke reviewed these provisions a few years later, he deemed Penn's standard too open-ended to be effective. These guidelines would spark "perpetual prosecution and animosity," Locke warned, because they were too loose to be enforceable.[16]

With somewhat different emphases, Penn and Locke were both concerned with the problem of civility—that is, with the need to have Christians bridle their tongues, that most insolent of human organs. In both Europe and America, a major front in the struggle for toleration involved the very language of religious polemics, whether delivered in writing or in the most casual of conversations. Time and again the free expression of religious beliefs easily degenerated into personal insult and doctrinal mockery, or what Bejan has called "the cesspools of religious insult, anonymous anathemas, and pamphlet outrage that characterized the early modern debates about religious toleration." Penn would have allowed government to monitor religious conversations in the cause of preventing casual yet provocative insults. By contrast, Locke wished to promote "a vision of *concordia* as the essence of toleration in a civil society, rather than of communion in the body of the church."[17]

Seventeenth-century America did not attain these high standards of *concordia*. In their own ways, Williams, Penn, and Locke were all visionaries, advancing the cause of toleration, yet still inhabiting a world where the active repression of disruptive beliefs and the regulation of worship remained plausible political options. Retrospectively we elide their differences in celebration of the greater good we want them to have pursued, but they might have balked at regarding themselves as collaborators in a common project. New York and Pennsylvania were not happy multicultural communities from the outset, but their settlement did create conditions in which sectarian toleration could develop. Still, had putative Domesday Book surveyors of the kind that Bernard Bailyn once imagined touring North America in 1689 made the state of religiosity a category of analysis, they could not have readily predicted that this colonial "marchland" would soon produce a historic departure in the fabric of church-state relations and the accompanying recognition of liberty of conscience as a fundamental, natural, and eventually a fully constitutional right.[18] The seventeenth-century colonies did *not* mark a radical break from English or European culture, except insofar as their mechanisms of population recruitment were already producing a strange intermingling of peoples.

## MAKING DISSENT AN ANACHRONISM

The conventional assumptions about the value of preserving religious orthodoxy and uniformity thus persisted into the early decades of the eighteenth century. Religious dissent was a form of disease or infection that authorities should quarantine or suppress. Tolerated dissenters should be restricted to worshipping quietly and privately. The legal privileges that dissenters gained were yielded grudgingly, mixed in with a fair dose of distaste and suspicion. Many, perhaps most colonists would have recognized that individuals possessed a right to private judgment of religious truth. But authorities still balked at permitting the open expression and publication of dissident opinions, and itinerant Baptists and Methodists still faced legal restrictions on their preaching.[19]

Yet by the middle decades of the eighteenth century, the colonists were beginning to inhabit a world of religious pluralism where law and custom were no longer strong enough to preserve communal uniformity and orthodoxy. The very idea of dissent was becoming problematic, as it became ever more difficult to say where orthodoxy resided. The idea that religion should become a matter, not merely for unending rounds of theological exposition and commentary, but for contentious public debate, became a commonplace. Perhaps most important, the idea that every individual's faculty for private judgment could also become a right of public expression became more compelling. There were multiple sources for this transition. Some of these sources reflected the distinctive characteristics of individual provinces and the doctrinal concerns of particular sects, especially in the aftermath of the first Great Awakening. Others echoed transatlantic currents and the emerging world of Enlightenment thinking, an intellectual world shaped by the ideas of Locke and Spinoza. This shift in sentiment was not an *event*, in the same way that the enactment of the Virginia Statute for Religious Freedom in 1786 marked a climactic moment in the separation of church and state. It was, rather, the culmination of a set of processes that together created the conditions that made the dramatic American departure possible.

One preliminary element in this shifting calculus was the evolving nature of imperial governance. This shift was particularly noticeable in Massachusetts Bay, the one colony that remained most committed to its original visionary impulses. In 1684 the first royal charter for Massachusetts was legally vacated. Two years later James II created the Dominion of New England, a new government whose rule eventually extended from the Jerseys through New York and all of New England. The existence of the Dominion threatened the

Puritan's grand errand of governing through godly commonwealths founded on the doctrine of religious covenant expressed through Congregational or Presbyterian principles. It also promised to give the Church of England full legality, or perhaps even supremacy, in the religious realm.

The Dominion collapsed after the Glorious Revolution of 1688, and King William granted Massachusetts, Connecticut, and Rhode Island new charters of government. The greatest change came to Massachusetts. The province now had a royal governor, and the right to vote in provincial elections no longer depended on full admission to a church, but simply on the secular norm of ownership of property. Anglicans could vote, too, and the province was legally bound to extend liberty of conscience to all denominations. Instead of renewing their errand into the wilderness, the second charter gave Puritans a lesser satisfaction: the reassurance that the essential structure of congregational governance they had established in the 1630s remained intact.

In a general sense, early eighteenth-century colonial religious life reflected the impact of the parliamentary Act of Toleration. Although that act was a flawed and partial measure, it nevertheless marked a modest step in the development of English religious freedom. It ended the arbitrary and cruel treatment to which Quakers, Baptists, and other dissenters had been subjected— although Presbyterian meetinghouses in England were still sacked "with alarming frequency."[20] Even if the Toleration Act operated mostly as a signal, even if Catholics enjoyed no new protection, a corner had been turned, and the persecutions of the past two centuries could pass into the realm of history. The Act did not legally bind Americans, but it did influence their behavior. Eighteenth-century America was a more *provincial* society than the original colonial settlements had been, and conforming to the new norms of British practice—what historians sometimes call the Anglicization of American culture—was one consequence of that process.

Yet if the Toleration Act operated as a signal of shifting norms, the more important developments were those that occurred within the provincial societies of British North America. Arguably the most dramatic of these took place in Pennsylvania. William Penn imposed a policy of religious toleration on his commonwealth, but he spent only a limited amount of time there. Like other "lawgivers" in antiquity—Moses gazing into Canaan from the heights of Har Nevo, Lycurgus going into exile from Sparta—he was effectively separated from the polity he founded. In Pennsylvania as in Europe, the real work of promoting active tolerance had to occur among the people themselves, in the communities where they settled, and within the denominations and sects they freely supported but sometimes abandoned.

For members of established churches, the disestablishment of religion in the colony posed significant challenges. Liberty of conscience was a noble principle, but how could a denomination preserve uniformity or orthodoxy when internal dissent arose, as it often did? How would churches used to relying on public funding cope in an environment where congregations had to be self-sufficient? The existence of a public regime of toleration made it difficult to oppose other sects with the fervor with which Europeans routinely denounced one another. Nor was there any way to compel lax or dissenting members to conform to church doctrines. Settlers increasingly worshipped in whichever church seemed most convenient, independent of their initial affiliations. The dispersion of individual farmsteads aided this free-floating distribution of adherents. It mattered, too, that economic ambitions outweighed religious commitments for many immigrants.[21]

With each passing decade immigrant newcomers acquired a better grasp of the logic of Pennsylvania's regime. "In effect, competition forced compromise," the historian Sally Schwartz observes; "to protect one's right to act in accordance with individual beliefs entailed a recognition that a similar right must be accorded to those with differing beliefs and practices."[22] Religious disagreements *within* individual denominations and sects mattered more than disputes *between* them. But collectively, multiethnic, multidenominational Pennsylvania was fostering the growth of an active culture of free religious expression, one that followed Quaker guidelines about the powerful role of conscience without indulging the ranting against false beliefs that made the original Quakers so obnoxious. To knowing observers, like the young James Madison in the 1770s (who pined for his annual visits to Philadelphia, perhaps to sate his secret craving for scrapple), the Pennsylvania approach seemed an exemplary success.

The twin prongs of Penn's recruitment strategy, with its dual reliance on religious freedom and economic opportunity, made Philadelphia a magnet for immigrants. Penn sent his agents to Ireland and the continent, drawing populations, like the Scotch-Irish Presbyterians fleeing the rent-racking practices of their Anglo-Irish landlords, who began filtering into other colonies, making their demography more complicated. The modernity of Penn's seventeenth-century "holy experiment" turned eighteenth-century Pennsylvania into "the best poor man's country in the world." As James T. Lemon's pioneering study of its historical geography argues, settlement patterns illustrate the inherent liberalism of its immigrants. Their decisions about where to live, what to plant, and when to move rested not only on rational economic calculations but also on their desire to live near their countrymen.[23] Yet one can also speculate whether Pennsylvania was also fostering another form of rights consciousness, one that made the exercise of religious conscience a deeply felt personal liberty. Just as William Penn had linked liberty of conscience to the other fundamental rights of political representation and trial by a free jury, so European immigrants may have begun to absorb a distinctively English conception of rights from the colony's enlightened policies.[24]

So Pennsylvania, more than New York, best foreshadows the American future of religious toleration. Not that the colony remained wholly free of religious strife. The question of whether Pennsylvania, with its dominant and pacifist Quaker party, should collaborate with imperial military policies sparked repeated controversies in the mid-eighteenth century. Anglican and Quaker leaders competed to recruit support from German and Scotch-Irish communities, and religious themes figured prominently in their appeals. Yet in a variety of ways, Pennsylvanians with different creedal faiths and ethnic origins were learning to interact harmoniously.[25]

The one development that had the most profound impact on American religious culture, however, was the set of mid-century revivals known as the Great Awakening. Scholars debate whether it is correct to synthesize the Awakening as one unfolding event, spreading its way across the colonies, or as a clerical "invention"—an artful campaign waged by preachers intent on promoting evangelical Christianity.[26] Broad agreement nevertheless remains about the impact of this burst of religious revivalism, both within individual denominations and across the American Protestant landscape. The Awakening provided vivid contrasts between two very different styles of preaching. One favored a "reasonable" Christianity readily accessible to ordinary parishioners, a body of belief shared by an array of confessions capable of respecting each other's sincerity. The other called for reviving the emphasis on human sinfulness in order to trouble listeners to confront their inner depravity and begin the whole process of conversion that would lead to a rebirth in Christ and thus to grace. Old Light or Old Side ministers, the exponents of a reasonable Christianity, were initially willing to let the acolytes of revival ply their craft. But New Light or New Side ministers were far less charitable. They actively disparaged the staid preaching of the settled ministry and challenged their audiences to reject uninspired sermons in favor of a more enthusiastic and spontaneous religion. It was the immediate, direct, overpowering experience of conversion, "rather than doctrinal knowledge or conformity to conventional practices," that stirred the awakened and altered their personalities.[27]

Revivalist preachers were often itinerants, some native to America, others sailing over from Britain. The most influential was George Whitefield, the Grand Itinerant, a founder of the new Georgia colony and a major proponent of the Methodist movement within the Church of England. Whitefield's grand tour in 1739–1740 was a genuinely inter-colonial event. Word of his coming ran in advance, and farmers would drop their tools to hurry to the meeting site, which was often an open field where Whitefield would preach atop his traveling stool.[28] No one was his rhetorical equal. Yet the impact of the Awakening hardly rested on Whitefield's accomplishments alone, but rather on the legions of itinerants he inspired, particularly as the message of conversion spread into the backcountry where organized churches were few and far between. Their preaching had a disruptive impact in countless communities, challenging the authority and convictions of settled ministers, inspiring open debates within contentious congregations, rupturing individual churches, and openly encouraging the reborn godly to worship with one another while spurning fellowship with their unregenerate neighbors. This contested state of belief proved a great source of bitterness and anxiety in mid-century America, igniting recriminations, resentments, and misgivings within families and communities alike.[29]

Yet that contested situation proved to be more of a transition than a lasting condition. There is no question that the Great Awakening broadened the spectrum of Protestant religiosity, multiplying theological perspectives and ecclesiological disputes while making it more difficult for individual denominations to maintain their cohesion. These sources of diversity were also augmented by the flow of immigrants from abroad and migrants within. Yet by the 1750s and 1760s, as Chris Beneke persuasively argues, the dominant impulses in American Protestantism were increasingly ecumenical and irenic in nature. Religious leaders were growing more inclined to emphasize the virtues of a Christian union that would embrace multiple denominations and to value the essential beliefs that should unite all Christians. Even the Awakening's most ardent leaders, Whitefield included, came to realize that recriminations against dead religion had gone too far. Implicit in this approach was a latitudinarian recognition that many points of doctrine were no longer worth contesting. By the early 1750s, Beneke observes, "orthodox Congregationalists, German Pietists, nonresisting (pacifist) Quakers, New Light Presbyterians, established Anglicans, and dissenting Baptists invoked the notion that essential beliefs would unite Christians of all types if the particular nonessentials that divided them were ignored or forgotten—and the essentials themselves were left sufficiently vague and capacious."[30]

This relaxation of confessional ardor and combativeness was reflected in the workings of other institutions. As the number of colonial newspapers multiplied, printers treated their columns as a neutral forum "Open to All Parties." The growth of clubs and fraternities, especially Freemason lodges, took place on wholly nonsectarian grounds. American colleges retained denominational connections and duties—notably training ministers—but their student bodies were not restricted to members of one denomination. The opening of new colleges—like New York City's King's College (later Columbia)—could spark disputes over sectarian governance, but so long as students conducted themselves in religiously respectful ways, they were free to pursue their own spiritual choices and commitments.[31]

The condition the provinces of British North America had generally reached on the eve of the revolutionary controversy no longer required colonists to learn to tolerate each other. The idea of toleration as it was traditionally understood—the burden of accepting offensive beliefs and behavior—no longer seemed pertinent. The quintessential right of conscience, the right of private judgment in matters of faith, was generally accepted. Nor was this a merely private right that dissenters could exercise only in the safe confines of their homes, in the same way that the parliamentary Conventicle Acts created a minimal secure space where families could worship as they wished. As the American pattern of church-state relations (outside Pennsylvania and Rhode Island) moved toward a hybrid form of multiple establishment in which all denominations enjoyed a measure of public support, the idea of religious dissent atrophied. All denominations operated on a plane of equality in which each should be free to pursue its own notions of ecclesiology. Thus when disputes arose over the desire of Anglicans to establish a colonial bishopric, which the fundamental tenets of their church logically demanded, their advocates did not rely on the inherent authority or superiority of an established church, but rather on the obligation of other denominations to respect the distinctive needs of their church. In a sense, Anglican representatives were asking religious groups once labeled dissenters to tolerate the detested prerogatives of an established church, to allow Anglicans to exercise the same religious liberty that dissenters already possessed.[32]

These conditions were coalescing in the American colonies on the eve of the revolutionary controversy. Much of the hard work of moving "beyond toleration" had already been done, not because that was a goal the colonists were consciously pursuing, but rather because an array of factors was converging toward that end. It mattered that the absence of Catholics—their status as an external enemy rather than an interior rival—eliminated the flashpoints that repeatedly disrupted communal peace in Europe. It mattered, too, that the recriminations the Great Awakening unleashed, and the turmoil that individual congregations and communities felt so deeply, did not lead to a lasting embitterment. There were modes of cooperation as well as conflict that came out of the mid-century upheaval. Perhaps equally important, the catalyzing role of itinerant preachers, carrying their message to terrain well beyond the reach of institutional religion, helped to ensure that the new American republic would retain a profoundly Protestant identity. Because so many of these preachers taught a Gospel of conversion nurtured by Baptist or Methodist convictions, they made every individual's claims for a sovereignty of conscience a paramount concern of daily religious life. Liberty of conscience mattered to Americans because that was something they were routinely urged to exercise, and to treat as a right they could never alienate.

So critical elements of the American approach to religious freedom were already available, were already maturing, on the eve of the revolutionary controversy with the British Empire. What remained to be determined was the place they would occupy in American constitutional thinking. That was the project that Thomas Jefferson and James Madison inherited, and which indeed formed one significant foundation of their lasting alliance, the most remarkable friendship in the nation's political history, and one that would have a lasting impact on its jurisprudence.

## CHAPTER THREE

# The Revolutionary Legacy
## *Jefferson's and Madison's Great Project*

WE CAN SPECULATE how American religious life might have evolved had the Revolution not occurred and the colonies remained in the empire. Some form of weak religious establishment could have persisted in many provinces. Imperial patronage could have given the Church of England modest advantages over rival denominations. Such establishments would nonetheless have been largely nonpreferential in nature. Any denomination wishing public support would have been able to receive it, while Quakers and Baptists could still have gone their voluntary ways. Most important, Americans would have maintained their principled commitment to the free exercise of religious conscience as a natural right. That right would not have been limited to the security of religious belief within the privacy of the home. It would also have protected the open forms of religious expression already witnessed in the first Great Awakening. The basis for a consensus of this kind was well established by the 1770s; it did not need the logic of rebellion to carry it forward.

Yet the Revolution did occur, and it did intervene, powerfully, in the ways in which Americans thought about the free exercise of religion and its constitutional relation to the protection of rights more generally. That intervention was inadvertent. The pursuit of religious liberty was not part of the revolutionary movement that led to independence. Yet once the states started drafting constitutions of government in 1776, questions about the relation of church and state and the religious rights of individuals began to matter. The Revolution enabled Americans not only to think systematically about the nature of religious freedom, but also to comprehend developments that had already taken place over the past century and a half. Rethinking the religion problem was one crucial facet of "the contagion of liberty" that accompanied the decision for independence.[1]

One mark of the importance of this idea lay in the central place that religious freedom occupied in the political thinking of Thomas Jefferson and James Madison. In their view, this was not one more right among many in a catalog of basic liberties. Nor was it wholly akin to the common-law procedures codified in the state declarations of rights. In the realm of religion, they believed, Americans had the opportunity to go further than other peoples—to go beyond Locke, or the exemptions of the parliamentary Act of Toleration, or indeed the concept of toleration itself. As Jefferson observed in the notes he compiled on Locke's *Letter Concerning Toleration* in the fall of 1776, "It was a great thing to go so far (as he himself sais of the parl. who framed the act of toler[atio]n; but where he stopped short, we may go on."[2]

Yet this pursuit of a broader conception of religious freedom mattered not only for its own sake, but also because it embodied a leading edge of American constitutional thinking. No other right placed as great a value on the moral autonomy of individuals, women and men alike, or on their capacity to shield their beliefs and behavior from the scrutiny of the state. No other right, therefore, placed as great a value on *privacy*, that complex concept that figures so prominently in modern discussions of liberty. No other right provided a better foundation for the main thesis of "the Madisonian constitution" expounded in *Federalist* 10 and 51: the belief that the best security for liberty would rely on the existence of a multiplicity of sects (or interests) that would cure the "mischiefs of faction."

Finally, the organic connection between the individual's free exercise of religion and the principle of disestablishment illustrated one further achievement of revolutionary constitutionalism. With other votaries of the social contract, Americans believed that a government exercised only those powers that the people had delegated to it. But this abstract belief did not really reduce the plenary legislative power that governments wielded. By contrast, denying government the power to support, enforce, or regulate religious behavior did constitute a significant reduction in the authority of the state. This was a power that no previous government would ever have abjured, because religion was too essential and volatile a matter to privatize. The movement toward disestablishment thus marked the single most important step that the revolutionary constitutionalists took to limit and cabin the scope of legislative authority.

From the vantage point of American *civil* religion—that larger body of attitudes and habits that maintain the stability of the republic—it also matters that Jefferson and Madison were the two most active acolytes of these ideas. The point is not to make them the sole or supreme representatives of the best American thinking on this question, but rather to understand why it mattered so much to them, and then to ask what we can learn by grasping its importance. To ask why the chief authors of the Declaration of Independence and the Constitution were so devoted to this cause provides a valuable point of departure for asking why religious freedom, in certain respects, became a right unlike any other—what made it so radically significant.

Jefferson was eight years Madison's senior. He attended the College of William and Mary, the second oldest institution of higher learning in British America, where he was treated (rightly) as his College's and perhaps the colony's brightest young man. His intellectual and cultural interests were astonishingly cosmopolitan. Fill out the potential titles for books on his many interests, and one could readily write about *Jefferson and Architecture* or *Food* or *Wine* or *Music* or *City Planning* or *Agriculture* or *Technology* or *Women* or *Education* or *Literature* or *Antiquity*, as well as all the topics relating to his public life. In the range of his interests, his only competitor was Benjamin Franklin, the luminary whom Jefferson replaced but could not "succeed" as the American minister to France.[3] Madison's interests were also broad but not quite so cosmopolitan. Rather than study in Williamsburg, he traveled to Princeton, where he fell under the tutelage of John Witherspoon, the newly arrived, evangelical Presbyterian president of the College of New Jersey. In their origins, Jefferson and Madison were two provincial intellectuals, reared on isolated plantations in central Virginia. But in their education and ambitions, they represented the leading edge of the various movements that we collectively call the American Enlightenment(s).[4]

In May 1776 the subject of constitution making engrossed both men. Jefferson, just turned thirty-three, was attending the Continental Congress in Philadelphia. But he badly wished to be back in Williamsburg, where the Fifth Provincial Convention was drafting Virginia's first constitution. The adoption of these new constitutions, Jefferson believed, had become "the whole object of the present controversy," a matter of such importance that he wished the convention would recall its congressional delegates so that they, too, could join the process.[5] Instead he was marooned in Philadelphia, to inherit the world-historical task of writing the Declaration of Independence. The opportunity of constitution making came instead to Madison, just turned twenty-five. He was a junior and deferential member of the Fifth Convention, but he did serve on the constitution-drafting committee chaired by George Mason, and he did intervene on the one matter that personally most concerned him: securing liberty of conscience.

Tracing the *intellectual* origins of their individual commitments to religious freedom is a complex matter, and not all the details of their youthful development need concern us here. A devastating fire at Jefferson's Shadwell plantation in February 1770 left him "utterly destitute" of his personal and legal papers, so we know little about his early religious sentiments.[6] By contrast, Madison's correspondence with his close friend William Bradford offers important insights into the religious thoughts of his early adulthood. Moreover, the intellectual environment he entered at Princeton has been the object of careful study, because President Witherspoon turned the College of New Jersey into the leading forum for disseminating the ideas of the Scottish Enlightenment. Witherspoon was an ardent Presbyterian who believed in the importance of individual spiritual regeneration rather than man's innate capacity to secure moral improvement. He also represented that wing of the Kirk of Scotland that favored liberating congregations from public control, and was thus receptive to the relaxed forms of establishment that flourished in America.[7]

One can actively debate whether or how deeply Madison's ultimate recognition of the multiple sources of factious behavior—the great vice of republican politics analyzed in *Federalist* 10—reflected or diffused the Calvinist emphasis on original sin he learned in college. However one assesses that relation, the definition and depth of his religiosity remain a "puzzle" shielded by his profound sense of privacy. His family worshipped within the Church of England, and Madison maintained that association throughout his life. Yet as Lance Banning has noted, "he never entered full communion or identified himself as an Episcopalian."[8] The letters he wrote William Bradford after returning to Montpelier in 1772 confirm that he was well learned in divinity and initially concerned "to have our names enrolled in the Annals of Heaven."[9] After Madison entered public life in 1776, however, references to his own religious life disappear. Was he a Unitarian? Was he a Christian in the orthodox sense of believing in the divinity of Jesus, or simply a deist? Did he believe in miracles or divine revelation? To these questions there are no positive answers. One might suppose that the absence of any overt religious expression is itself a tacit form of repudiation, because religiously devout individuals are rarely quiet about their convictions. Or perhaps the absence of such references only evinces Madison's conviction that religious matters should remain deeply personal and private.

Yet Madison was never silent about his commitment to religious liberty. The strongest early expression of this came in a January 1774 letter to Bradford, when he denounced the recent local confinement of half a dozen Baptist preachers "for publishing their religious Sentiments which in the main are very orthodox." This exercise in "That diabolical Hell conceived principle of persecution" drove the somewhat priggish college graduate to distraction. "I have neither patience to hear talk or think of any thing relative to this matter, for I have squabbled and scolded abused and ridiculed so long about it, [to so lit]tle purpose that I am without common patience." What Virginia badly needed was not toleration for dissenters but full acceptance of "Liberty of Conscience."[10] In April 1774 Madison feared that an expected effort of "the Persecuted Baptists" and

Presbyterians to attain "greater liberty in matters of Religion" at the imminent meeting of the Virginia assembly was likely to fail. Virginia lacked "That liberal catholic and equitable way of thinking as to the rights of Conscience" that were "the Characteristics of a free people," like Bradford's fellow Pennsylvanians. Like other enlightened observers, Madison thought religious freedom would promote other progressive tendencies such as "Industry and Virtue," "Commerce and the Arts," and the "Love of Fame and Knowledge." It was both a product of enlightenment and its source.[11]

Jefferson sat in the legislature that received the Baptist petition in April 1774, but news of the Boston Port Act quickly disrupted its session. Two more years passed before Virginia political leaders confronted the religion question directly. When they did, it was Madison's youthful commitment that led to the important change in the Virginia Declaration of Rights that moved the commonwealth beyond toleration to the true principle of religious liberty.

The story is a familiar one. The relevant article proposed by George Mason's constitution-drafting committee reflected the broad consensus that Americans shared. Article XVI held "That religion, or the duty which we owe to our Creator, and the manner of discharging it, can be directed only by reason and conviction, not by force or violence; and therefore, that all men should enjoy the fullest toleration in the exercise of religion, according to the dictates of conscience, unpunished and unrestrained by the magistrate," unless some overt act disturbed the civil peace. Madison prepared two revisions to this article, which he asked two more senior members to propose. The first, introduced by Patrick Henry, stated that "all men are equally entitled to the full and free exercise" of religion "according to the dictates of conscience," and further held that "no man or class of men ought, on account of religion, to be invested with peculiar emoluments or privileges." The former clause shifted the discussion of religious freedom from a toleration yielded by the community to the idea of an inherent right possessed by all. The latter clause was effectually an attack on the legal establishment of the Church of England and thus raised other questions of religious policy that the convention did not wish to confront. This proposal was accordingly rejected.

Madison's second revision, however, did pass muster. Introduced by Edmund Pendleton, it preserved the definition of religious freedom in the first draft and then added that its exercise would remain "unpunished and unrestrained by the magistrate, unless the preservation of equal liberty and the existence of the State are manifestly endangered." In the language of modern jurisprudence, the "manifestly endangered" phrasing of this second proposal would have subjected any regulatory activity by the state to the *strictest scrutiny*. Rather than go that far, the convention eliminated any reference to the residual supervisory power of the state.

Jefferson had also included a religion clause in the three drafts of a Virginia constitution he prepared while he was attending Congress. In his wording, "All persons shall have full and free liberty of religious opinion; nor shall any be compelled to frequent or maintain any religious institution." In the original drafts, Jefferson included a clause enabling the magistrate to prosecute "seditious behavior" or "seditious preaching or conversation against the authority of the civil government."[12] That clause, like the equivalent language in Madison's revision, also disappeared. Religious freedom had to be proclaimed on its own terms, for its own sake. If other civil problems ensued, they would be dealt with separately. Notably, Jefferson included his statement of rights in the text of his constitution, not in a complementary declaration of rights.

There is much to be said for the literary economy that Madison and Jefferson favored. Both preferred simple statements that treated conscience and free exercise as unequivocal fundamental rights. The comparable statements of religious freedom that appeared in other state constitutions were more complex and therefore more susceptible to interpretation. Article XVI of the Virginia Declaration became a signal for further reform. In the early 1770s, the religious dissenters who petitioned the House of Burgesses were still seeking specific exemptions for their own sect or church or minister. In 1776 the tenor of their petitions quickly shifted. Rather than seek exemptions or indulgences or a bare toleration, Chris Beneke observes, calls for religious freedom became more spirited, as "the groveling language of indulgence gave way to the emboldened language of liberty and equality."[13] This demand became more evident as new petitions demanding disestablishment began flooding the Virginia assembly.

Those petitions helped to form the original basis of the half-century friendship of Jefferson and Madison. Freshly returned from Philadelphia, Jefferson joined the committee on religion to which these petitions were referred, and Madison was also one of its members. The debates within the committee and assembly were intense and divisive, and they produced no immediate consensus in favor of disestablishment. The completion of that half of the project would take another decade. Jefferson, who had little fondness for heated debate, later called this episode "the severest contests in which I have ever been engaged." Yet amid this dispute he also undertook his own research program, examining Virginia's laws on religion, reading about the history of episcopacy and heresy, and perhaps most important, thoroughly reviewing Locke's *Letter Concerning Toleration*. It is easy to imagine Jefferson and Madison discussing this research and agreeing on its essential conclusions.

Jefferson's reading notes of 1776 are detailed and learned. Jefferson the classicist was always happy to dabble in the original Greek, as his notes on episcopacy, which relied on Paul's epistle to Timothy, reveal.[14] He took care to define theological tendencies and heresies in Christianity, distinguishing the doctrines of the

Council of Nicaea (325 C.E.) as well as the beliefs of the Sabellians, Socinians, Arminians, Arians, Apollinarians, and Macedonians, especially as these related to the existence of the Trinity and the divinity of Jesus.[15] Perhaps most important, the notes on Locke's *Letter* are not a routine summary of a text already well known, but a fresh and inquisitive assessment of its relevance to the American situation. Locke had done much, Jefferson realized, "but where he stopped short, we may go on."

The initial efforts of Jefferson and Madison to reform the regulation of religion in their native state met only mixed success in 1776. Jefferson's bill to disestablish the Church of England was rejected in committee. Dissenters were left free to withhold their contributions to the established church. But the possibility remained open that a general assessment in favor of all sects could still be enacted. Madison's success in converting the religion article of the Declaration of Rights into a principled statement of free exercise remained a powerful symbol of the state's commitment—but it was only that. Taken alone, Madison feared, Article XVI did *not* provide an adequate or comprehensive security for religious liberty. Should a popular or legislative majority will it, established religion could be maintained and the rights of dissenters narrowed. To go effectually beyond Locke thus required more than an assertion of principle. It also meant rethinking the very nature of a constitutional right, and thus understanding how the religion question was related to other incipient aspects of American constitutionalism.

## THE PROBLEM OF PROTECTING RIGHTS

Article XVI contained a concluding clause that we have not yet quoted: "that it is the mutual duty of all to practice Christian forbearance, love, and charity, towards each other." To the modern mind it is difficult to read this clause as a statement of a right. We may have a moral or civic *duty* to treat others with "forbearance," but how such a duty becomes a right to be invoked against the authority of the state is virtually inconceivable. Yet to the adopters of the Virginia Declaration, this view was unproblematic. Such a declaration was viewed less as a catalog of legally enforceable claims than as a collection of principles designed to guide the behavior of officials and citizens. Of course, these documents did list a number of common-law procedures that governments were urged to respect. Yet these clauses were often expressed with a monitory "ought" rather than an imperative "shall" acting as the operative verb. Other rights declared were also more political than legal in character. Advising citizens to return officials to their "private station" through rotation in office was a political principle, not a constitutional rule.[16]

The early declarations of rights were legally problematic in one other sense. In Pennsylvania and Massachusetts, these declarations were incorporated in the text of the constitution and thus acquired legal force. But elsewhere these declarations stood as separate documents accompanying the promulgation of a constitution but devoid of any legal authority. They embodied principles that republicans ought to respect rather than rules anyone had to enforce. For a fundamental right to be fully constitutionalized, in the sense in which we use that term, it had to become an organic part of a constitution. That status in turn depended on the evolving definition of a constitution—on determining whether it was a supreme fundamental law, for example, or the equivalent of a super-statute subject to later legislative amendment. This was a question that Jefferson and Madison both took very seriously. The path that leads from Article XVI of the Virginia Declaration to the Religion Clause of the First Amendment thus traced a new arc in American constitutional thinking.

After 1776, Jefferson made the conversion of republican principles into a modern legislative code his chief task. That was the guiding animus of the committee he chaired on the revisal of Virginia laws. Many of these bills provide essential insights into his thinking, but arguably the most important was Bill 82, the Statute for Religious Freedom. Along with the Declaration of Independence, and the creation of the University of Virginia, this was one of the three achievements Jefferson had recorded on his cenotaph at Monticello. There was a time when he thought the most important bill was his plan for public education, which was, in special ways, linked to his ideas of religious reform. But that bill was never enacted, while the Statute for Religious Freedom, with Madison's active shepherding, was finally adopted in January 1786.[17]

Each of the three paragraphs of the Bill for Religious Freedom forms a distinct text in itself and a text that modern readers might well find puzzling. The first and by far longest paragraph—the preamble—provides an extended moral, religious, and political justification of the act. The second paragraph is the actual statute. It simply states

> that no man shall be compelled to frequent or support any religious worship, place, or ministry whatsoever, nor shall be enforced, restrained, molested, or burthened in his body or goods, nor shall otherwise suffer, on account of his religious opinions or belief; but that all men shall be free to profess, and by argument to maintain, their opinions in matters of religion, and that the same shall in no wise diminish, enlarge, or affect their civil capacities.

The final paragraph then adds one further reflection on the legal status of the act. Because no legislature can ever bind its successors, some future assembly could easily revoke the statute. But should that repeal occur, "such act will be an infringement of natural right."

Whole chapters can be written about this act, and a wonderful collection of scholarly essays celebrated its bicentennial.[18] The most complex facet of interpretation involves the preamble, because here Jefferson invoked multiple principles and sources of authority to establish the rationale for the act. "Almighty God hath created the mind free," and "the opinions and beliefs" that define our individual religious identity can never be compelled by the magistrate or enforced "by temporal punishments, or burthens, or by civil incapacitations." That was "the plan of the holy author of our religion" who could have coerced both body and mind, but who instead chose "to extend [his plan] by its influence on reason alone." When the House of Burgesses debated this text, Jefferson recalled, some members proposed identifying Jesus Christ as "the holy author," but that amendment was roundly rejected, allowing the act to bring everyone under "the mantle of it's protection." In 1786 the Virginia senate did delete Jefferson's invocation of "reason alone," which offended Calvinist notions of conversion depending on the implantation of divine grace. But the larger claims remained intact.

Jefferson's conception of religiosity retains a fundamentally Protestant character. True religion remains a matter of inner conviction, not outward conformity, and men and women attain that condition voluntarily. The state has no capacity to regulate these convictions. Its "legislators and rulers, civil as well as ecclesiastical" are "themselves but fallible and uninspired men," with no superior ability to attain religious truth. The magistrate can always punish "overt acts against peace and good order." But the matters of opinion that religious faith ultimately represents are just that: ideas subject to "free argument and debate; errors ceasing to be dangerous when it is permitted freely to contradict them."

Why did Jefferson write this rhetorically ingenious paragraph? A modern reader might expect to find language like this in a resolution celebrating some patriotic event or praiseworthy action. But in a statute meant to have concrete legal effect? Yet in the eighteenth century, most legislative acts were not conceived as broad statements of public policy. They typically addressed particular petitions and requests coming from individuals and communities. When a legislature enacted a general public law of this kind, however, a measure affecting the entire society, attaching a justificatory preamble remained entirely appropriate. What sets Jefferson's preamble aside is less the nature of its objectives than its author's moral commitments. Equally important, the preamble, even with its extraordinary length, echoes the ways in which the conventions for stating a fundamental right still entailed the endorsement of its underlying principles. The legal authority of the statute depended on the requirements of the second paragraph, but its effectiveness also depended on inculcating the values of the preamble.

Yet one other problem still remained, as the strange concluding paragraph made clear. Jefferson's statute would clearly advance the project he and Madison had launched. Once it was adopted, religion would be effectively disestablished in Virginia. No one could be taxed or compelled to support any denomination, church, or teacher of religion. Unless you stood outside the church window and hollered blasphemous thoughts during the sermon, thereby disrupting the peace, no one could be punished for heretical or merely heterodox ideas, because those subjects would legally cease to exist. Yet once adopted, the bill would still be subject to later legislative modification or repeal, even if that action violated the natural right that Jefferson had just explained—a right that was truly natural because it reflected an innate quality of the human mind.

It was a standard trope of eighteenth-century thinking to argue that the kinds of natural rights invoked, say, by Locke did become subject to legal regulation and thus modification once a compact of government was formed. But the Jefferson-Madison project had a further goal: to minimize the sphere of legal regulation as much as possible by turning religion into a private matter. That could not be wholly accomplished *legally*, because statutes were always subject to revision. But it might be done *constitutionally*, once one found a way to make a written constitution the supreme law of the land.

The development of that concept was a central achievement of revolutionary constitutionalism, and Jefferson and Madison were essential contributors to that process. Jefferson wrote an important passage on this subject in his *Notes on the State of Virginia*, dwelling on the multiple meanings of the word *constitution*. It was not the *definition* of constitution that mattered, Jefferson argued, but the procedures used to make it legally superior to ordinary statutes. If such a mechanism did not exist, the familiar maxim of *quod leges posteriores priores contrarias abrogant* (later laws contradicting earlier laws, abrogate them) would intercede.[19] Massachusetts, after four years of controversy, had solved this critical problem in 1779–1780 by having a special convention frame the constitution that its town meetings, articulating the voice of popular sovereignty, then ratified. Jefferson and Madison hoped that Virginia would call a fresh convention to revise the state's constitution, but that option never materialized.

At the close of the war for independence, then, the movement for disestablishment in Virginia was still incomplete. Indeed it faced a new challenge, because within the legislature, there was substantial interest in levying a general assessment that could be used, on a nonpreferential basis, to support ministerial salaries throughout the state. That measure was formally introduced at the fall 1784 session of the legislature, and it enjoyed the support of the state's leading orator (or demagogue, depending on one's point of view), Patrick Henry. Episcopalians predictably favored it, but more surprisingly, Presbyterians reversed their prior position to support it as well. After being term limited out of the Continental Congress, Madison had returned to the legislature in 1784, and quickly became its most active and influential member. But on this occasion, with the assembly narrowly divided, discretion seemed the better part of valor. The measure was too important, Madison protested, to be adopted without ample public discussion. With a bit of maneuvering, Madison managed to delay the final reading of the bill for a full year.

Madison's most important public discussion of religion, his *Memorial and Remonstrance against Religious Assessments*, was prepared during that interval and circulated as a petition. The suggestion to draft this anonymous petition came from George Mason. Notwithstanding his seminal contributions to *The Federalist*, Madison was a reluctant public polemicist, and four decades passed before he acknowledged his authorship.[20] More than Jefferson's preamble to the Statute for Religious Freedom or his chapter on religion in *Notes on Virginia*, the *Memorial* remains the central statement of the enlightened approach to religious freedom that the sages of Monticello and Montpelier pursued, and it deserves careful examination.

The opening paragraph of the *Memorial*, which begins by quoting Article XVI of the Declaration of Rights, is arguably its most important. Here Madison sounded recognizably Lockean notes. Every person's religion is a matter of individual "conviction and conscience." The exercise of freedom of conscience is an "unalienable" right, for two reasons. First, religion itself being a matter of opinion, "depending only on the evidence contemplated by their own minds," no one can alienate its exercise to "the dictates of other men." Second, it is also unalienable because "what is here a right towards men, is a duty towards the Creator." Everyone must determine individually what "homage"—or, more expansively, what forms of faith and worship—the Creator deems "acceptable." So far, so good: Madison was essentially restating the basic argument for the sovereignty of conscience that Locke, following many other writers, had made. Yet Madison then extends this argument in a seemingly radical way. "This duty is precedent, both in order of time and in degree of obligation, to the claims of Civil Society." Before one becomes "a member of Civil Society," he is already "a subject of the Governour of the Universe" who cannot sacrifice the "allegiance" he owes "to the Universal Sovereign."

Read broadly, this paragraph seems to allow individuals to seek exemptions from any of a number of legal requirements. In an influential article on "The Origins and Historical Understanding of Free Exercise of Religion," the distinguished constitutional scholar and jurist Michael McConnell gave just such a reading to this claim. In this area, McConnell argues, Madison's attitudes diverged from Jefferson's and Locke's positions in important ways. "Consistent with this more affirmative stance toward religion, Madison advocated a jurisdictional division between religion and government based on the demands of religion rather than solely on the interests of society."[21] That claim is highly relevant to constitutional jurisprudence today, when demands for exemptions from an array of regulatory acts dominate the agenda of religious freedom. But how well does this bold interpretation of Madison's argument meet the context in which he was acting?

Two puzzles immediately intervene. The first concerns Madison's concept of the chronology of human belief. What can it mean to make religious duty "precedent" in time to one's civil obligations? For Locke, a profound philosopher of education, religious convictions clearly developed over time, were something that a child would be incapable of choosing, and a subject that required mature consideration. The self-determined nature of one's religious duty had to evolve and cohere as one matured; it hardly existed as an *ex ante* condition that preceded one's civil status. Jefferson's ideas of public education, which were a main part of his republican agenda, rested on similar assumptions. Teaching the Bible in public schools would become acceptable, he argued, only after students had first read history. Until they acquired historical knowledge, they would be incapable of making any informed religious choice of how churches had actually operated. And that history, as Jefferson regarded it, was not a happy tale. The more history one knew, the more skeptical one would become of the self-serving claims advanced by so many denominations. Christianity itself would rank high, perhaps highest, on his roster of moral culprits. "Millions of innocent men, women, and children, since the introduction of Christianity, have been burnt, tortured, fined, imprisoned," Jefferson wrote in his *Notes on Virginia*, "yet we have not advanced one inch toward uniformity."[22] Too much religious history was a story of priestcraft and oppression!

It is difficult to see, then, how religious duties somehow preceded civic ones. Any child was always a subject of duly enacted laws before he or she had fashioned a religious identity. The question of when children could plausibly give their consent became, as Holly Brewer has demonstrated, a compelling matter in religion, politics, and law. But in each of these realms, prevailing ideas began to recognize the prior mental dependence of children.[23] Madison must thus have had some other conception in mind in asserting the priority of religious duty. It is not the *superiority* of religious claims to secular ones that distinguishes his case for the duty we owe the Creator, but rather the *nature* of religious obligation itself. Here it is difficult to see how or why Madison would have felt driven to explore new ground, that is, to offer a broad theory of religious exemption from civil law when the subjects that Virginians were disputing remained conventional objects of controversy. For historians, context is everything, and the context of debate in 1784–1785 was quite familiar. No one then was imagining the ambit of the modern regulatory state or the multiple points where its reach would intersect or conflict with private religious conviction. The general assessment bill traversed well-trod ground, and so did Madison.[24]

Where the *Memorial and Remonstrance* did innovate was in trying to reconcile the familiar argument over public support for religion with the evolving assumptions of republican constitutionalism. Madison ended the important first paragraph by posing a genuine puzzle: "True it is, that no other rule exists, by which any question which may divide a Society, can be ultimately determined, but the will of the majority; but it is also true that the majority may trespass on the rights of the minority." This is the statement of a problem for which Madison as yet had no solution. The dominant paradigm for eighteenth-century thinking about rights presupposed that the real challenge was to protect the collective body of the people against the concentrated authority of the government, and particularly against the unitary power of the executive. Representative legislatures were viewed as rights-protecting institutions, conceived to ensure that laws regulating ordinary behavior were enacted with popular consent, not imposed on a docile population. The idea that a legislative majority could enact laws inimical to the rights of minorities was not itself a novelty. That was a story that historically informed Americans could readily recall from Parliament's seventeenth-century Conventicle and Test Acts, as well as from the wretched abuse of the Quakers. But the idea that the majority in a *republic* devoted to rule by the people could act this way was something of a discovery. It also posed one of the key problems that preoccupied Madison's creative political thinking over the next few years: the problem of the "factious majority" governing in defiance both of public good and private rights.

Madison pursued these concerns in ensuing items of the *Memorial*. The second paragraph linked the existence of a natural right of religious belief held by people in society to the resulting limitation on the power of government in general and the legislature in particular. The third paragraph invoked the "prudent jealousy" that "the free men of America" had shown at the outset of the Revolution with the need to secure religious liberty *now*. The revolutionaries "did not wait till usurped power had strengthened itself by exercise, and entangled the question in precedents. They saw all the consequences in the principle, and they avoided the consequences by denying the principle."[25] In the fourth paragraph Madison grounded his position on the principle of equality. Each subject entered society "on equal conditions," with the same capacity to embrace or reject religious ideas. That equality would be eroded, Madison argued, with an ironic twist, if self-sufficient groups like the Quakers and Mennonites gained an advantage over other sects by showing that "their piety alone" sustained "public worship" without the crutch of public support.

This observation provided a transition to a broader subject: the corrupting effects that formal ties between church and state imposed on both, a corruption that the evidence of history again amply demonstrated. There was no evidence that "the Civil Magistrate is a competent Judge of Religious Truth," Madison wrote. If religion became "an engine of Civil policy," it would create "an unhallowed perversion of the means of salvation." The true history of Christianity proved that "this Religion both existed and flourished, not only without the support of human laws, but in spite of every opposition from them," sustained only by "its own evidence and the ordinary care of Providence." Conversely, "experience witnesseth that ecclesiastic establishments" nearly always led to "pride and indolence in the Clergy, ignorance and servility in the laity, in both, superstition, bigotry and persecution." Similarly dismal results came when an established church supported civil government, for then "in no instance have they been seen the guardians of the liberties of the people."

Echoing Jefferson's Query XIII in the *Notes on Virginia*, Madison provided the same grim view of the human costs of the search for religious uniformity.

> Torrents of blood have been spilt in the old world, by vain attempts of the secular arm, to extinguish Religious discord, by proscribing all difference in Religious opinion. Time has at length revealed the true remedy. Every relaxation of narrow and rigorous policy, wherever it has been tried, has been found to assuage the disease. The American Theatre has exhibited proofs that equal and compleat liberty, if it does not wholly eradicate it, sufficiently destroys its malignant influence on the health and prosperity of the State.

Madison's reference to "the American Theatre" can be read as an eighteenth-century counterpart to John Winthrop's "city on a hill"— a testament not to the ideal church polity that the Puritans once sought, but rather to an ideal definition of the relation of church and state, or more directly, to the barrier or wall between them.

Madison's fifteenth and final point returned his analysis to the central problem of defining and protecting rights. Here he again echoed Jefferson, latently invoking the logic of the final paragraph of the Statute for Religious Freedom. The free exercise of religion "is held by the same tenure with all our other rights." But equal tenure also meant equal vulnerability: "Either then, we must say, that the Will of the Legislature is the only measure of their authority; and that in the plenitude of this authority, they may sweep away all our fundamental rights," Madison concluded, "or, that they are bound to leave this particular right untouched and sacred."

In effect Madison was challenging the central premise of constitutional thinking that made the legislature—not the judiciary—the chief protector of the rights of the people. The entire analysis of the

*Memorial and Remonstrance* was thus bracketed by two momentous puzzles: one asking how the majority of the people could act in violation of rights, the other challenging the familiar presumption that the legislature's chief duty was to secure the rights of the people against the arbitrary power of the state. When he wrote the *Memorial* in the late spring of 1785, Madison had no obvious solution to either problem. He had not yet formulated his concept of the "factious majority": a majority claiming the political right to rule, but lacking the normative capacity to pursue either the public good or private rights. Nor did he yet have any ready answer to the problem that had also stumped Jefferson: how to prevent one errant legislature from undoing the good deeds performed by its predecessor. But he was beginning to identify those problems, and soon he fashioned noteworthy solutions that reshaped American constitutional thinking.

### FROM JEFFERSON'S STATUTE TO THE RELIGION CLAUSE

The *Memorial and Remonstrance* was not the only petition circulating against the assessment bill, nor even the most influential. Other petitions gained more signatures. But this net expression of the public opinion of the commonwealth proved decisive. When the assembly convened in October 1785, the assessment bill proved dead on revival. In the wake of its rejection, Madison moved ahead to secure the enactment of Jefferson's revised code of laws. When his legislative earnestness began to grate his colleagues, he insisted that the Bill for Religious Freedom stay on their agenda. When the senate moved to eliminate Jefferson's stirring preamble, Madison worked to reinstate it, conceding a few alterations too minor to oppose. After the measure was finally adopted in January 1786, Madison recounted these maneuvers to Jefferson, and then ended his account with this fulsome compliment: "The enacting clauses [that is, the second paragraph] past without a single alteration, and I flatter myself have in this country extinguished for ever the ambitious hope of making laws for the human mind."[26]

Nearly a year passed before Jefferson answered this letter, but he certainly agreed with Madison's sentiments. He had already taken steps to have the Statute translated and distributed as widely as possible in Europe. Jefferson, too, believed that the free exercise of religion implicated more than the rights of belief and conscience. "It is honorable for us to have produced the first legislature who has had the courage to declare that the reason of man may be trusted with the formation of his own opinions," independent of the "vassalage" previously imposed "by kings, priests & nobles."[27]

Of course, other mechanisms continued to curtail the free expression of some opinions, even in the constitutional monarchy of Britain and the American republics. Seditious libel against government was still punishable, and remained controversial in America through the 1790s. But in Jefferson's imagination and Madison's, the expression of religious opinions was a harbinger for a broader enlightenment. Once blasphemy became a problematic legal concept—an offense that was rarely prosecuted even as freethinkers were multiplying— could the erosion of seditious libel be far behind? The free expression of religious opinion could thus become paradigmatic of public speech more generally. It was religious animosity far more than political repression that had produced the slaughter of innocents that Jefferson and Madison detested. And when states did act violently, were not religious animosities, rather than political or dynastic commitments, the chief source of their cruelty? Solving the religion problem in this way might thus promote the transition to a society that would be more civil and enlightened than its fervent antecedents.

The outcome of the Virginia debate over the assessment bill should thus have heartened Madison. An appeal had been made to the voice of public opinion, and the citizens of Virginia had taken the side of religious freedom. The state passed Jefferson's visionary statute, truly a landmark piece of legislation. Yet in the period immediately following this success, Madison's seminal thoughts on the protection of rights grew more, not less troubled. Much of this mounting concern in... in his fears about the popularity of paper money, a policy that threatened the fundamental rights of property. But the religion question remained a puzzle as well, and Madison continued to mull its significance as he framed his agenda of constitutional reform.

Not long after Madison drafted the *Memorial and Remonstrance*, he wrote a long letter to a college friend in which he laid out his criticisms of the state constitutions. The shortcomings of "the legislative department" marked the initial item on his agenda. "If it were possible it would be well to define the extent of the Legislative power," he wrote, "but the nature of it seems in many respects to be indefinite." Nevertheless, Madison listed some "essential exceptions," nearly all of which involved individual rights. Religion headed this list. "The Constitution may expresly restrain them from medling with religion," he began, before citing two other fundamental civil rights, jury trial and habeas corpus, which the Anglo-American legal tradition valued deeply. The key shift is that Madison saw the legislature as the source of danger. The key reservation was that the plasticity of legislature power, its supple ability to deploy "an infinitude of legislative expedients," made this power so difficult to blunt or contest.[28]

Yet in the realm of religion, simple statements might actually work. A strong affirmation of the individual right to the free expression of religion, a forthright denial of the state's capacity or obligation to support religious institutions, would create bright-line zones of security. The same clarity could never be applied to protecting rights of property, simply because the scope of legislative action

would inevitably affect different classes of property holders in complex ways. In the realm of other common-law rights tied to subjects'
involvement with magistrates, judges, and juries, there was ample
room for interplay between courts and legislatures. Such rights were
procedural in nature, and therefore subject to recurring legal refine-
ment and adjustment. The realm of religious belief and behavior
was significantly different. For all the nuances and complexities of
religious doctrine—all those everlasting disputes over soteriology
and ecclesiology, baptism and communion, transubstantiation and
*adiophora*, the crucifixion and resurrection of a living god immacu-
lately conceived—religion itself could be safely privatized, *if* one
conceded that everyone had an equal right to his or her opinion on
these subjects and that this right was a universal property that all
were commonly obliged to respect. For freedom of conscience and
other essential rights were faculties that one *owned*. Man "has a property of peculiar value in his religious opinions, and in the profession
and practice dictated by them," Madison wrote in 1792. "In a word,
as man is said to have a right to his property, he may be equally said
to have a property in his rights." Among these rights, "Conscience
is the most sacred of all property; other property depending in part
on positive law [legislation], the exercise of that, being a natural and
unalienable right." Conscience was a right even "more sacred" than
treating "a man's house as his castle."[29]

The genius of the Madisonian constitution lay in generalizing
this notion of the inherent diversity of religious opinions protected
by rights of conscience to the general problem of republican government. Turn American's Protestants loose with their Bibles, unleash
the free exercise of their opinions, Madison supposed, and there
would be no end to their disputes and the sectarian divisions they
would foster. In the realm of religion, the best security for personal
liberty would inhere in the existence of a "multiplicity of sects"; in
the larger realm of civil rights, in a corresponding "multiplicity of

interests." Madison's appreciation of the political benefits of religion did not depend on the moral virtues it would foster among its votaries and acolytes. He made this point quite explicitly in the concluding item of his April 1787 memorandum on the "Vices of the Political System of the United States." Would religious convictions deter individuals from committing or supporting acts of injustice, Madison asked? Individuals often freely violated their religious commitments, and when they participated in some collective misdeed, even when under oath, they would "join without remorse in acts, against which their consciences would revolt if proposed to them under the like sanction, in the security of their closets." In its enthusiastic moments, religion could be a destructive passion; "in its coolest state," it could also "become a motive to oppression." The republican benefits of religion were thus due, Madison concluded, not to the moral virtues it taught citizens, but to the inadvertent advantages of sectarian diversity.[30]

Madison continued to mull these issues after the Constitution was drafted. He repeated the observations about religion recorded in "the vices" memorandum in his important letter to Jefferson of October 24, 1787. He revisited the religion question a year later, when he sent Jefferson a lengthy explanation of his begrudging willingness to add a declaration of rights to the Constitution. Madison did not believe that the adoption of a bill of rights was important for its own sake, and lingering concerns about freedom of conscience illustrated his reservations. Unlike the Virginia Declaration of 1776, which the provincial convention had simply promulgated, a constitutional amendment would now have to secure some form of ratification reflecting the sovereign voice of the people. That worried Madison, because "I am sure that the rights of Conscience in particular, if submitted to public definition would be narrowed much more than they are ever likely to be by an assumed power" wielded arbitrarily by government. Here Madison cited the claims of New

England Anti-Federalists that the constitutional prohibition on religious tests in Article VI "opened a door for Jews Turks & infidels" to gain public office.[31]

The better lesson came from Virginia, however, and it confirmed Madison's view that declarations of rights were only "parchment barriers" that "overbearing majorities in every State" had repeatedly violated. Thanks to Madison, the Virginia Declaration included a strong statement of religious freedom, later reinforced by "the additional obstacle which the law has since created" with Jefferson's Statute. Yet had the legislature discovered, back in 1785, that popular opinion did favor a new "religious establishment," or had a single denomination, in some burst of enthusiasm, converted a majority of the population, Article XVI of the Declaration would lose its authority and the legislature would readily reverse its position on the Statute for Religious Freedom, just as Jefferson feared it might, natural right be damned.

The explanation of this point carried Madison's thinking about the protection of rights down a different path from the one that Jefferson still favored. In a typically brief but seminal statement, Madison reformulated the whole problem of republican rights:

> Wherever the real power in a Government lies, there is the danger of oppression. In our Governments the real power lies in the majority of the Community, and the invasion of private rights is *cheifly* to be apprehended, not from acts of Government contrary to the sense of its constituents, but from acts in which the Government is the mere instrument of the major number of the constituents. This is a truth of great importance, but not yet sufficiently attended to: and is probably more strongly impressed on my mind by facts, and reflections suggested by them, than on yours which has contemplated abuses of power issuing from a very different quarter.

Jefferson had spent the last four years in Paris observing the abuse of power by an absolutist monarchy, while Madison was sorting out the vices of republican government at home. Much of his concern rested on his fear of the popularity of paper money; but as this letter also attests, the religion problem remained in the forefront of his thinking, as a paradigmatic example of the problem of protecting rights in a republic, where the people themselves would rule.

Like so many other aspects of his constitutional thinking, Madison's thoughts about the protection of rights had a further complexity and nuance that modern readers often miss. By October 1788, as his letter to Jefferson confirms, he favored adding a set of rights-protecting clauses to the Constitution. His commitment on this point, however, rested more on political calculations than constitutional values. He still did not believe that a constitution lacking some statement of rights was materially defective. He thought instead that a body of well meaning if somewhat misguided citizens existed whose qualms about the Constitution would be allayed by the adoption of such clauses. Yet if he could persuade the First Congress to offer such amendments—a circumstance he did not take for granted[32]—it should do so in a way that would maximize their legal effect. Most of the provisions that formed the core protections of the eventual Bill of Rights would thus appear in Article I, Section 9 of the Constitution, as restraints on the legislative authority of Congress. In pursuing this strategy, Madison was thus moving beyond the dominant understanding of 1776, when rights-protecting clauses were regarded more as freestanding principles than as legal injunctions. His approach to amendments amounted to giving claims of rights a fully constitutional and positivist status. (In the end Roger Sherman got the better of this debate, and Congress proposed the amendments as supplemental articles, rather than interwoven clauses.)

Yet there was another sense in which Madison's approach reflected a traditional notion of how bills of rights would actually operate. Although he wanted to enhance their legal authority by directly embedding these statements in the constitutional text, he doubted that courts would have the temerity to enforce these protections against the political will of a dominant legislature and the impassioned popular majority it represented. In a monarchy, he wrote Jefferson, "a solemn charter of popular rights" would work among the people as "a standard for trying the validity of public acts, and a signal for rousing & uniting the superior force of the community" against the coercive authority of a state. In a republic, however, "the tyrannical will of the sovereign" resided in the people themselves. Should interest or passion or religious or racial prejudice stir them to some unjust action, a bill of rights would be a mere parchment barrier—nice to read, but difficult to apply.

Yet Madison did envision one potential long-term application of a bill of rights. In one of his many remarkable passages that distills a powerful thought into a single sentence, Madison asked "what use then . . . can a bill of rights serve in popular Governments?" His two answers to this question both relied on the educative, rather than legal, value of a bill of rights. His second answer imagined that even in a republic there might be occasions when the people as a whole had to be rallied against an oppressive government. But his first answer matters more for our concern with the religion problem: "The political truths declared in that solemn manner acquire by degrees the character of fundamental maxims of free Government, and as they become incorporated with the national sentiment, counteract the impulses of interest and passion." A constitutional commitment to "the rights of Conscience in their fullest extent" would work best by inculcating norms and attitudes that would mitigate the evils of religious prejudice and sectarian antipathy. By making the free expression of religion a civic norm, citizens and denominations would grow more enlightened, more tolerant, in their dealings with each other, and less inclined to use legal mechanisms to advance their sectarian concerns and interests. This educative role of a bill of rights would thus provide a prospective cure for the "mischiefs of faction" that he denounced in *Federalist* 10, that seminal statement of "the Madisonian constitution."

Yet in Madison's way of thinking, the dangers of factious majorities were more likely to be felt, and to persist, at the state and communal levels of government. That was why the one provision he valued most in the amendments he presented to Congress on June 8, 1789, would have added to the restrictions that Article I, Section 10 imposed on the state legislatures an additional clause holding that "No state shall violate the equal rights of conscience, or the freedom of the press, or the trial by jury in criminal cases." The House approved that clause, but the Senate rejected it.

The eventual Religion Clause of the First Amendment had a more complicated history. In the original form that Madison gave it in June 1789, it had three main ends. First, it would prevent the abridgement of any individual's civil rights "on account of religious belief or worship." Second, it would prohibit the establishment of "any national religion." Third, it would declare that "the full and equal rights of conscience" shall not "be in any manner, or any pretext infringed." After further committee proceedings and a desultory debate, the House of Representatives adopted a more concise clause: "Congress shall make no law establishing religion or prohibiting the free exercise thereof, nor shall the rights of conscience be infringed." On September 9 the Senate amended the clause to read: "Congress shall make no law establishing articles of faith, or a mode of worship, or prohibiting the free exercise of religion." These terms would preclude any effort to define a national religious orthodoxy, but other forms of establishment—like the nonpreferential logic of the Virginia general assessment bill—would remain permissible. The House rejected this language on September 21, while naming Madison, Sherman, and John Vining to the conference committee it appointed to work out its differences with the Senate. That committee notably included the nation's first Roman Catholic senator, Charles Carroll of Carrollton (Maryland). The Religion Clause now took its final, extremely concise form: "Congress shall make no law respecting an establishment of religion, or prohibiting the free exercise thereof." Whatever "establishment of religion" meant, it now implied something more than the mere articulation of articles of faith or modes of worship. By contrast, the free exercise of religion necessarily subsumed the liberty of conscience. How could one ever exercise religion freely if rights of conscience were neither the source nor the objective of one's spiritual concerns?[33]

Language as spare as this would necessarily require further "liquidation," to adapt a term Madison used in *Federalist* 37 to explain how even the most carefully discussed laws would require "a series of particular discussions and adjudications" for "their meaning [to] be liquidated and ascertained." Generations would pass before federal courts began to "liquidate" the meaning of the Religion Clause, and when they did, Jefferson's and Madison's ideas figured prominently in their treatment. Because Madison's general theory of the extended republic still dominated his political thinking, the exact wording of the Religion Clause probably did not trouble him very much in the summer of 1789—*unless its language was drawn too narrowly*, as the Senate proposed, so that it would reduce rather than broaden the working scope of the constitutional right. We have no record of the conference committee's rapid deliberations, but it is impossible to imagine Madison not playing a dominant role on a question that had agitated his entire life. It is entirely proper to regard the Religion Clause as Madison's text and Jefferson's legacy.

## A MATTER OF EMPHASIS

There were nevertheless some striking differences in emphasis that distinguished the two Virginians' modes of thinking. One remarkable aspect of their half-century friendship was that their general consensus on political objectives did not keep them from disputing other points. Their minds worked in different ways, and so did their pens. Jefferson wrote with more enthusiasm and spontaneity, while Madison was more inclined to distinctions and qualifications. As Madison observed of Jefferson, not long after his death, "allowances ought to be made for a habit in Mr. Jefferson as in others of great genius, of expressing in strong and round terms, impressions of the moment."[34] On many issues, Jefferson expressed "strong and round" opinions that Madison labored to modify.

Religion was one of those questions where they agreed on essentials but differed over details. Jefferson really hoped that broad principles of religious freedom and open debate would gradually turn Americans—or at least the predominant Protestants—into Unitarians. The more freely they debated the great issues of Christian theology in a society where the state lacked the power to preserve orthodoxy or punish heresy, the more enlightened Americans would become. The mysteries of the Trinity would be forgotten; Jesus could be recognized (as Jefferson regarded him) as a sublime moral prophet, but not a god in human form who performed miracles; and the rigid doctrines of Catholicism and Calvinism could be dismissed as mere theological scholasticism. The university that Jefferson proudly founded in nearby Charlottesville would have no need for a professor of theology or a chapel for students. Americans could openly welcome immigrants from other cultures and religions. Their religious beliefs and opinions might not merit equal respect with the essential Christian values Americans already shared: Jefferson shared the common eighteenth-century view that Islam had conquered more by force than persuasion.[35] Yet he was also part of an Enlightenment world that took the study of religiosity as a matter for anthropological analysis and rational comparison.[36] In the final analysis, Jefferson believed that all religious faith was essentially a matter of opinions no one could prove.

It was thus a great disappointment to Jefferson to live long enough to realize that a reasonable Unitarianism might not secure a dominant position in American culture. By his providential death on the fiftieth anniversary of the Declaration of Independence, he could observe the gathering force of the Second Great Awakening, that powerful revival which the revolutionary settlement of the religion question had done so much to liberate. The upsurge of evangelical Christianity manifested in the surging popularity of Baptist and Methodist churches did not evoke a cry of hallelujah from Jefferson. Here again, as in so many aspects of his life, one has to confront Jefferson's inherent complexities. On the one hand, he welcomed the political support he received from religious dissenters who joined his struggle against the existing establishment. Yet he hardly celebrated the revival of a militantly evangelical and Pentecostal culture that could never reduce religious belief to a mere matter of subjective opinion.[37]

Madison's position was far more philosophical—or rather, far more content with the evolving characteristics of American religion. He left no record of his reactions to the spiritual currents swirling through the post-Revolutionary United States. He left later scholars ample space for speculation and little room for documentation about his religious beliefs. But on the public consequences of the fruits of disestablishment and the acceptance of free expression, Madison was unequivocal. The great question had been put to a historical test in various American states—and especially in Virginia—and the results of the experiment were beyond dispute. In defiance of the received view "that Civil Govt. could not stand without the prop of a Religious establishment, & that the Xn. religion itself, would perish if not supported by a legal provision for its Clergy," Madison wrote in 1819, "The experience of Virginia conspicuously corroborates the disproof of both opinions." Civil government was doing just fine, "Whilst the number, the industry, and the morality of the Priesthood, & the devotion of the people have been manifestly increased."[38] Madison was theologically indifferent to the competing claims of rival sects. Unlike Jefferson, he did not worry whether religious sentiments were growing more reasonable or enthusiastic, more predestinarian or Unitarian. The compelling lesson was that Virginia's religious experience confirmed the hypotheses of *Federalist* 10 and 51: a multiplicity of sects (or interests) in an amply sized republic would cure the mischiefs of faction and promote the rights of minorities and individuals. That was all the wisdom he needed.

There were thus some differences in the ways in which the sages of Monticello and Montpelier thought about religiosity. But on fundamental constitutional matters their convictions converged. Both imagined a republic where religion was wholly privatized, where individuals were free to form their own convictions and nurture their own doubts, where churches were mere voluntary societies relying on the free contributions of their members, where the state lacked authority to foster orthodoxy or punish heresy. Jefferson would have permitted laws punishing Sabbath-breaking to preserve the peace of the community, yet he and Madison also believed that closing the post office on Sunday amounted to an establishment of religion. One way or another, the observation of the Sabbath was too much a part of the texture of American life to be wholly ignored. But in every other respect, they envisioned a society where matters of religion were solely dependent on the complete autonomy of individual citizens, and where the state could effectively remove religion from the realm of public regulation. In their own ways, these were founding principles of American constitutionalism.

## CHAPTER FOUR

# The Democratization of Religious Freedom

THE FAMOUS STATEMENTS of Jefferson and Madison provide the *locus classicus* for the American constitutional ideal of religious freedom. In its first landmark ruling on free exercise, the Mormon case of *Reynolds v. United States* (1879),[1] the Supreme Court relied on Jefferson to distinguish a protected realm of belief from other provinces of behavior (in this case, polygamy) that remained subject to legal regulation. Even if skeptics rightly caution against turning the beliefs of the two friends from Albemarle and Orange counties into a constitutional orthodoxy, their joint commitments to religious freedom remain notable because of their extraordinary influence on American political thinking.

Yet when Americans defined their conception of religious freedom in the decades after the adoption of the Constitution, they turned neither to the succinct phrasing of the First Amendment nor to the Virginia Statute. Their favored text was instead the Pennsylvania constitution of 1790, which trimmed down the language that state had initially adopted in 1776.

That all men have a natural and indefeasible right to worship
Almighty God according to the dictates of their own consciences;
that no man can, of right, be compelled to attend, erect, or support any place of worship, or to maintain any ministry against
his consent; that no human authority can, in any case whatever,
controul [*sic*]or interfere with the rights of conscience; and that
no preference shall ever be given, by law, to any religious establishments or modes of worship.

The new constitutions of Kentucky (1792), Tennessee (1796), Ohio
(1803), Indiana (1816), Illinois (1818), Missouri (1820), Arkansas
(1836), Texas (1845), and Wisconsin (1848) adopted this language
with only slight variations. Much more than the lean text of the First
Amendment, this consensus best illustrates how post-Revolutionary
Americans understood the free exercise of religion.

What principles of the free expression of religion does this language effectively endorse? First, the free exercise of conscience is
a natural right that no one can forfeit or alienate, and a right that a
written constitution can confirm though not create. Second, the protection of that right extends beyond mere matters of belief. It also
frees the individual from any obligation to participate in or to support
any church or ministry. Third, no institution can compel any form
of religious behavior, which individual conscience alone can dictate.
On the free exercise side of the equation, the Pennsylvania language
offers an unambiguous endorsement of individual autonomy and the
free right of individuals to choose their religious affiliations.

The most important consequence of this consensus was the creation of the booming spiritual marketplace that defined nineteenth-
century American religiosity. The withdrawal of the state from the
active support and regulation of religion inspired churches and
ministers to compete for adherents and individuals to choose their
affiliations. Individuals joined and left churches as they wished. In

some areas, like the Burnt Over district of upstate New York, the cacophony of religious voices made it ever more difficult for earnest truth-seekers to adjudicate the contending spiritual claims. To the familiar desire of Protestants to experience the conversion of the rebirth in Jesus, the Second Great Awakening offered another form of conversion: the active movement of individuals from one denomination—or sometimes one faith—to another.[2]

The creation of this religious marketplace was part of the post-Revolutionary democratization of American culture, a process best captured in Alexis de Tocqueville's classic volumes. It was not only American culture that was democratized, however, but religion, too, as Nathan Hatch explains in his great book, *The Democratization of American Christianity*. The "mass movements" of the Second Great Awakening had a "populist" dimension, Hatch argues. American Protestants turned "away from central ecclesiastical institutions and high culture," giving "unschooled and unsophisticated" citizens "a marvelous sense of individual potential and of collective aspiration." American ministers could not afford to act as snobby protectors of their own gentility. Instead they "pursued people wherever they could be found; embraced them without regard to social standing; and challenged them to think, to interpret Scripture, and to organize the church for themselves."[3] It was the dawn of an evangelical age that made Americans arguably more religious than their colonial antecedents had been.

This transformation affected the free expression of religion in three momentous respects.

First, the formal separation of church and state could never wholly separate the realm of religion from the dominion of law and governance. Churches often aspired to act as moral communities that sought to resolve disputes among their members and enforce religious norms of behavior. Yet they often turned into contentious gatherings that had to resolve their own internal disputes by resorting to law. Churches owned property and collected income; they required some rules of internal governance; they had quarrelsome members and ministers who expected that many of the controversies between pulpit and pew needed legal resolution. The work of disestablishment could not be completed by simple constitutional fiat or a wholesale abandonment of legal authority. Legislatures and courts still had roles to play in regulating the contours of religious life. Even more important, as Sarah Barringer Gordon has argued, they defined the legal conditions on which the enterprise of disestablishment would proceed.[4]

Second, the success of this evangelical errand produced a new if more diffuse form of a Protestant establishment: a "moral establishment," as David Sehat has called it, which in turn created a perceived need for a "second disestablishment."[5] The renewed sense of Christian morality that drove the energetic reform movements of the antebellum decades had legal and political consequences. Profoundly religious values affected and inflected a wide array of concerns: antislavery, temperance, family law, education, blasphemy, and sexual expression. To comply with the accepted norms of disestablishment, these movements could not advance the doctrinal commitments of particular denominations. They instead worked to form a broadly ecumenical consensus that united most Protestant denominations. The best example of this consensus lay in the realm of education. It was perfectly legitimate to read the Bible to schoolchildren as a universal source of human morality, so long as teachers offered no interpretive commentary on the holy text.

But which Bible was one supposed to read? At the turn of the nineteenth century, "English-speaking Christian biblical critics almost all considered the Bible a unitary source of timeless truth: a single, inspired 'Sacred Volume' unique among ancient texts." By mid-century, the work of German academic critics was shattering that belief.[6] But at the level of popular culture, the conventional view remained that the King James Bible—the text that school-children listened to, or which they read at home or in church—was the authoritative rendering. The challenge to its preeminence came not from learned biblical critics versed in German scholarship, but rather from Catholics who rejected the entire Protestant conception of how children should be taught the Bible, and who instead used the Douai text originally translated in 1582 by English Catholics. Their repudiation of the Protestant consensus challenged the idea that a plain reading of the Bible was consistent with Americans' underlying commitment to disestablishment.

By 1850 the once minuscule Catholic population now formed a visible and vocal component of American society, its numbers swelling with migrations from Germany and a famished Ireland. Church leaders were never supplicants at a Protestant shrine. They shared the reactionary attitudes that characterized the nineteenth-century Church, and they still treated Protestants more as dissidents and heretics than companion seekers of common Christian truths. They failed to share the egalitarian perceptions that enabled most Protestant denominations to celebrate the pluralism of American religiosity. Many Protestants' perceptions of the insidious dangers of an expanding Catholic presence reflected age-old images of Catholic tyranny, rooted in *Foxe's Book of Martyrs* and generations of denunciatory sermons.

Starting with the so-called Bible war waged in Ohio in 1869–1873 and continuing down to the mid-twentieth-century debates about public support for parochial education, the growth of sectarian schools raised difficult questions about how religious truths could be presented in a public forum. Under the rubric of the Religion Clause or its state-based alternatives, however, this question related more to problems of establishment than to free exercise, and thus illustrated both the complicated ways in which the concept of religious establishment has continued to evolve in the United States, and the permeable boundary between a public establishment and the private expression of religious belief. To many modern legal commentators, a danger of establishment arises whenever public authority seems to endorse beliefs or practices associated with a particular faith, or alternatively, whenever individuals invoke religious scruples to seek an exemption from the requirements of civil law. In this understanding, seemingly minor matters, devoid of any obvious theological content, can treat a modest accommodation recognizing the free exercise claims of a religious group as a harbinger of a religious establishment.

Of course, the historical linkage of the Catholic Church with the coercive power of the state underlay the fears of nineteenth-century American Protestants. In the realm of free exercise, however, the true challenge came not from Catholics carrying the ideology of a reactionary Roman church, but rather from the native-born Church of Jesus Christ of Latter Day Saints. Relying on the ostensible discovery by Joseph Smith in 1829–1830 of a new revelation in the "golden plates" of the Book of Mormon that he deciphered with the aid of a "seer stone," Smith propounded a new theology that superseded Christian truth. As Chris Beneke argues, the Mormons, with their new dispensation, did not wholly accept the pluralism that characterized American culture: "Like Catholics, Mormons operated with the formal assumption that theirs was the one, true, and universal church," rejecting the common belief that a general acceptance of the core elements of Christianity united other denominations even when they disagreed over other particular issues.[7]

Equally important, the Mormons' early adoption of "the Principle" of plural marriage was an innovation that other Christians deemed profoundly offensive. Along with the evils of chattel slavery, the Mormon practice of polygamy constituted one of "the twin relics of barbarism" that transgressed the moral contours of society, a behavior too shocking and salacious to be viewed as a simple expression of sectarian difference. Because their exodus to the Utah territory left Mormons subject to federal jurisdiction, the ongoing struggle over "the Principle" ultimately became the basis for the critical case of *Reynolds v. U.S.* (1879), where the Supreme Court gave its first comprehensive account of the meaning of the free expression of religion by holding that the government could constitutionally prohibit the "barbaric" practice of polygamy.

## THE POST-REVOLUTIONARY ENVIRONMENT

In the first years after the adoption of the Constitution, it was not evident that the United States would soon develop a profoundly religious culture. An enlightened skepticism that had little interest in doctrinal orthodoxy was present in late eighteenth-century America. The intellectual advantage seemed to be shifting to the secular and the skeptical rather than the devout and the orthodox. Many of the nation's Founders shared the Deist sentiments that this attitude supported. While accepting of Christian moral beliefs, they were uninterested in miracles or revelation, and wholly indifferent (in the modern sense) to pointless theological disputations. Like Jefferson, many were amenable to Unitarian convictions. Influential voices of infidelity like Thomas Paine and Ethan Allen espoused a form of reason quite different from John Locke's *Reasonableness of Christianity*. Paine's *Age of Reason* and Allen's *Oracles of Reason* inspired freethinking readers in countless communities to challenge conventional religious belief. Even if many of these freethinkers were local oddballs, their mere presence in a society where heresy and heterodoxy were no longer punishable was threatening enough.[8] True atheism remained a rare phenomenon, but active disbelief was now evident.[9]

Post-Revolutionary American Christianity faced another threat that was itself revolutionary in nature: the great transformation that erupted in France in 1789. With its violent turn against the Catholic Church, the disorder of the French Revolution—"a cautionary tale of disestablishment run amok," Sarah Gordon notes—reminded many Americans of the value of traditional religiosity.[10] As President Washington famously observed in his Farewell Address, in language drafted by Alexander Hamilton, "let us with caution indulge the supposition, that morality can be maintained without religion." Perhaps "the influence of refined education on minds of peculiar structure" could secure that end among an educated elite, but "reason and experience both forbid us to expect that National morality can prevail in exclusion of religious principle."[11] The mass of mankind needed the moral discipline that religion provided. Locke would have readily agreed.

Hamilton wanted to add another query to this paragraph: Does national morality "not require the aid of a generally received and divinely authoritative Religion" as well? The final Address dropped this latent reference to Christianity. From the start of his presidency, Washington happily declared that the federal government was indifferent to citizens' religious identity. As he told the Tauro synagogue of Newport, Rhode Island, in August 1790, quoting the congregation's own statement back to them, "All possess alike liberty of conscience and immunities of citizenship. It is now no more that toleration is spoken of, as if it was by the indulgence of one class of people, that another enjoyed the exercise of their inherent natural rights."[12] Although Washington, the survivor of many a battle, believed that an ineffable Providence had guided his own life, his theological commitments were too weak to go as far as Hamilton's original sentence proposed.

When Washington visited Newport in 1790, the first ten amendments to the Constitution were not yet ratified, nor was it yet clear whether they ever would be. His sentiments represented general principles more than a specific reading of a constitutional text. Most Americans believed that the nation had moved "beyond toleration," making religious dissent a legally vacuous idea. Calvinism was still legally established in Massachusetts and Connecticut, but its persistence there was more a tribute to the weight of history than a harbinger of a future state. Yet the reaction against the excesses of the French Revolution, coupled with alarm over subversive freethinkers and skeptics, led members of different denominations to agree that they had common cause in promoting traditional religious values. Doctrinal differences mattered, but only up to a point. While eager to assert their own doctrinal claims, they conceded the bona fides of other denominations. If their practice of religion was fully protected, if there were no fruits of public support to be mustered, they need not regard rival denominations as hostile actors.

The existence of this latently ecumenicist consensus, this inter-denominational mutual recognition pact, was a precondition for the Second Great Awakening. It enabled different churches and sects to treat their spiritual competitors as rivals, not enemies. Like many mass religious phenomena, this great revival had multiple causes. The reasons why Americans sought spiritual rebirth, the psychological anxieties and earnest concerns that opened them to revival, were many and complex. Constitutional scholars have no need to measure these factors. But they do need to reckon with the decisive fact of American religious life in the new century. The consensus about the free expression of religion produced a dynamic competition among mainstream denominations and the insurgent dissenters who were busy purveying their own notions of salvation and ecclesiology.

With the states having lost their power to regulate religion, the results of this competition depended on the strategies and strengths of the rival churches and the desires and decisions of their prospective adherents. Different denominations had their own models of corporate organization and strategy. The two leading competitors were the Methodists, who descended from the Church of England, and the Baptists, who can be called radical Congregationalists. One would never want to confuse the hierarchical structure of the Methodists with the decentralized localism of the Baptists. Yet forms of corporate organization mattered far less than the enthusiasm of the salesmen and women who traveled cross country, whether they were ordained Methodist ministers or lay Baptist preachers, or the ordinary converts who zealously testified at the camp meetings that Methodists perfected, but which other sects also adopted. Under the stern generalship of Bishop Francis Asbury, young Methodist circuit riders traveled thousands of miles, often preaching their way to early deaths, presumably followed by a happy reception in the world to come. Revival meetings added a new dimension to popular religious performances. They often inspired a nearly anarchic spontaneity among the participants, and they dismayed many settled ministers who preferred the decorum of traditional sermons. But the fervor of camp meetings was also enormously empowering to the lay audience who were transported by the religious passions they released.[13]

Arguably the one great truth to be derived from this experience was that Madison, far more than Jefferson, got it right. Disestablishment had brought none of the adverse results its critics had predicted. Denominations freely marketed their beliefs, individuals freely chose their affiliations, and the corruptions of priestcraft had evaporated. Personal opinions of religious truth were left to flourish or wither, prodded by the reading of Scripture, the preaching of sermons, the leavening of revivals, and the free exchange of ideas. Although the experience of personal conversion disrupted the lives of many families,[14] Americans collectively respected their mutual rights of decision. This spiritual exchange had not produced the rational religiosity that Jefferson, sounding one of his many Pollyanna notes, had imagined.[15] Yet it fulfilled the enlightened dream of creating a society in which religion was no longer a source of overt conflict or persecution.

This idea of a spiritual marketplace did not mean, however, that religious groups were simply borrowing and adapting commercial modes of behavior to spiritual life. Rather, the legal reorganization of religious life actually placed local churches at the forefront of the growing use of the corporate form. Just as relaxing the prosecution of divine blasphemy anticipated the decline of the doctrine of seditious libel against government, so the use of corporate charters to organize religious societies preceded the emergence of the American business corporation. The benefits of incorporation had been granted to some religious societies before 1776, but mostly to established churches. No dissenters needed to apply. But with disestablishment, incorporation was no longer a privilege that the state selectively extended to one denomination, but a legal right that any qualified claimant could exercise.

New York set the key precedent. Article XXXVIII of its 1777 constitution struck a rhetorical blow against priestcraft by denouncing "the spiritual oppression and intolerance, wherewith the bigotry & ambition of weak & wicked priests & princes have scourged mankind." Seven years later, the legislature enacted a statute allowing all religious societies to gain the rights of incorporation. "Upon registration with the courts—not the legislature," Kellen Funk explains, "the trustees would become a body corporate capable of holding property, existing perpetually, and suing in court." Much as the Pennsylvania constitution's religion article became the model for disestablishment, the New York act set the precedent for the corporate organization of churches. This form of incorporation vested legal authority not in a denomination or synod or ecclesiastical hierarchy, but in trustees of a local congregation situated in a particular community. In a sense, the congregational model of church polity developed by the Puritans was becoming the dominant legal norm of American religious societies.[16]

Yet trustees did not always agree, ministers divided as well as united their congregations, and harmonious churches easily degenerated into hostile factions. The enthusiastic convictions that bound a church at its incorporation could grow controversial with the ebbs and flows of religious opinions and passions. In a litigious country like the United States, these disputes inevitably became objects of judicial scrutiny, and courts had to puzzle out ways to resolve rival claims.

Arguably the most important judicial holding in this realm of litigation came in *Dartmouth College v. Woodward* (1819),[17] one of the Marshall court's epochal decisions. Like other colleges, Dartmouth had religious origins and commitments. But after 1800 its curriculum became the object of extensive public controversy. Although it was a private institution governed by a group of self-perpetuating trustees, the College received significant support from the state, and this gave its affairs an openly political dimension. After 1804 a significant fraction of the faculty and students took a revivalist turn toward religious orthodoxy, in the process minimizing the authority of the college's venerable president, Eleazer Wheelock. In response, some of the state's Republican politicians argued that the orthodox faction at Dartmouth were part of a sinister campaign to reestablish religion in defiance of liberal (and Jeffersonian) principles. After carrying the 1816 elections, the Jeffersonians enacted a law altering Dartmouth's governance, including adding nine new members to the board of trustees, all to be appointed by Governor William Plumer, and creating a board of overseers who would preempt much of the work previously done by the trustees.[18]

The legal case began when the College's original trustees sought to block these changes. Eventually the case reached the Supreme Court. Oral argument in a packed court began on March 19, 1819, and consumed a good three days, with Daniel Webster, in full rhetorical flower, representing the College in its resistance to the state. The Court's holding in *Dartmouth* is distinctive in several respects. First, it extended previous decisions holding that state legislatures could not alter the legal rights duly vested in a corporation. That position derived not only from the Contract Clause of Article I, Section 10, but also from the Court's prior decisions in *Fletcher v. Peck*[19] (the 1810 decision relating to the Yazoo land fraud) and even more directly, from *Terrett v. Taylor*,[20] an 1815 decision involving an effort by the state of Virginia to recover lands previously granted to the Episcopal Church. Second, and far more important, the logic of *Dartmouth* created a strong distinction between a private realm of religious behavior, manifested in the College's original charter, and civil institutions explicitly created and sustained by the government to fulfill broad purposes of public policy. The fact that New Hampshire had later extended public support to Dartmouth did not alter or dilute the property rights vested in its original charter. The state retained the option to charter other institutions, designed under more republican principles—including a broader commitment to religious freedom—to attain these objectives. (Mr. Jefferson's own University in Charlottesville was conceived to launch such an enterprise.) But Dartmouth had been founded on other, more manifestly religious grounds. Its trustees, not the legislators, were the rightful determinants of its mission as "a private eleemosynary institution."[21]

In a clash between public authority and a private religious institution, American law would thus prefer the legal rights of the religious society to the legislative powers of the state. To subordinate questions of religious policy to the constraints of other legal doctrines, such as the law of trusts, amounted to finding a reasonably neutral way to assess the conflicting claims. But the nature of trusteeship was itself an important matter, and here, too, American law had to develop doctrines that were consistent with the general commitment to disestablishment. These doctrines in turn amplified the American understanding of the free exercise of religion.

When church trustees or congregations disagreed over matters of theology, they naturally turned to the courts. In pleading their clashing claims, they inevitably appealed to history and Scripture to justify their positions, placing courts in the awkward situation of having to assess vexed matters of biblical interpretation and the confessional legacies of the Reformation. Such examinations could produce hefty records of religious research. In one important New York case, *Gable v. Miller*,[22] the initial trial examination record ran to 250 pages "respecting the characteristics of the Calvinistic and Arminian doctrines, and the tenets respectively held by the German Reformed, the Dutch Reformed and the Lutheran churches." In his opinion, the deciding vice chancellor in turn cited the "significant differences between the Heidelberg Catechism and the teaching of Ulrich Zwingli" to demonstrate that Lutheran ministers could not be doctrinally excluded from occupying German Reformed pulpits. On appeal, first to the state chancellor, and then to the New York Court of Errors, this examination of theology and ecclesiology produced "over six hundred pages of Reformation theology, with citations to many significant Protestant reformers, confessions, catechisms, and church historians." Nor was *Gable v. Miller* a "unique" case, Kellen Funk concludes. "From 1830 until the Civil War, nearly every divisive point of Protestant theology likewise came into court with a request to enforce a charitable trust, including sabbatarianism, trinitarianism, the inheritability of sin, and the real presence of Christ in the Eucharist."[23]

A critical appraisal of this litigation supports two somewhat contradictory conclusions. One vindicates the core Madisonian proposition about religious freedom: turn Protestants loose with the Bible, leave them free to propound and sustain their views, and allow the resulting multiplicity of sects and denominations to secure the religious liberty of all. On the other hand, the disestablishment of religion could never wholly free the state from the legal duty of resolving the conflicts. In a good faith effort to adjudicate the claims laid before them, magistrates would have to resolve contentious matters of religious controversy, notwithstanding the fundamental position—propounded by Locke, Jefferson, and Madison—that the magistrate lacked any superior knowledge or capacity to resolve theological questions. Of course, in this case the magistrate was act- ing not as an instrument of public policy or as an agent or auxiliary of an established church, but was instead proceeding as a judicial authority dutifully bound to adjudicate cases and controversies. Even so, how could religion be considered as disestablished if doc- trinal claims remained subject to legal review?

The emerging American conception of disestablishment dealt with this challenge in several complementary ways. One involved recognizing the inherent difficulties of asking courts to resolve doc- trinal disputes. Rather than treat church trustees as agents strictly bound by the intentions and obligations prevailing at the moment when a church was incorporated—motives that could be tested under the rules of probate law—trustees should instead be regarded as corporate directors whose primary responsibility lay to their con- gregants. Church trustees, acting on behalf of a majority of their congregants, could thus make decisions much as trustees of other kinds of corporations would do.

This understanding in turn built upon practices that were embedded in the original legislation making church incorporation possible. As Sarah Barringer Gordon has argued, the process of dis- establishment imposed significant limits on the resources and gov- erning procedures of churches. State legislatures capped the amount of property churches could hold and the annual income they could receive. Over time these conditions were relaxed, but the early law of disestablishment was clearly designed to prevent American churches from acquiring the wealth that dissenting Christians had long found so distasteful in the Church of Rome or, for that matter, the Church of England. More important, the statutory regime made American churches subject to lay governance. It was the congregants, not the hierarchy or the ministry or the synod or the episcopacy, who retained primary legal authority. The animus underlying this policy was less anti-clerical than anti-corporate. It was not designed as an assault on the spiritual authority of the preaching class, but rather expressed the suspicion that the colonists had already directed against the monopolistic power and political influence of the East India Company, and that American citizens would again vent against the Second Bank of the United States, through the bully pulpit of President Andrew Jackson.[24]

This emphasis on lay governance did not discourage Methodists from developing a network of bishoprics or Mormons from creating a highly disciplined hierarchy. Even so, the authority that the use of incorporation gave to lay trustees marked an important development in the free exercise of religion. In ordinary legal usage, the incorporation statutes referred to churches as "religious societies," and thus echoed, perhaps knowingly, the language of Locke's *Letter Concerning* Toleration. "*Let us now consider what a Church* is," Locke had written. "A Church then I take to be a voluntary Society of Men, joining themselves together of their own accord, in order to the public worshipping of God, in such a manner as they judge acceptable to him, and effectual to the Salvation of their Souls." This idea of a church as a "free and voluntary Society" marked a historical departure from Christian practice, at least since the fourth century, but it also anticipated the working definition that Americans would accept.[25] Nor was this notion limited to Protestant churches.

The same enthusiasm for lay control that flourished in Protestant congregations infected their Catholic counterparts. Of course, the Church of Rome had a millennium and a half of hierarchical experience behind it, and in the nineteenth century its dominant ideology and sentiments often took a reactionary, anti-democratic, and anti-Rome turn. "The principle of trustee control over American churches compelled Rome to label trusteeism a heresy," Gordon notes, making it in fact "the only heresy ever to emerge from the United States." But Catholic congregants shared many of the sentiments of their Protestant neighbors. If they did not yet regard churches as free and voluntary societies, they still welcomed the evolution of mechanisms of lay control, or at least influence, within their parishes.[26] Their participation illustrated how aspects of the free exercise of religion cut across the most important denominational line of all: the boundary between Catholic and Protestant.

## THE MORAL ESTABLISHMENT OF A PROTESTANT REPUBLIC

This practice of organizing religious societies as chartered corporations was thus a significant milestone in American law. Here, as in other areas, laws regulating religion were not some incidental or derivative category of jurisprudence; in certain respects they proved fundamental to legal development more generally. This initial notion of religious incorporation had nothing to do with the question that bedevils American constitutional law today: whether private profit-seeking entities retain some right to the free exercise of religion. Incorporation secured the legal stability and autonomy of religious societies, yet it also gave the states a mechanism for managing disestablishment.

The Second Great Awakening had a second, more momentous impact on law. It generated an age of social, cultural, and political reform that sought to alter essential aspects of American life. Anti-slavery, temperance, a militant Sabbatarianism, and restrictions on gambling were all the beneficiaries of the moral impulses that evangelicals released. The impulse to rely on religion to improve morality was hardly a nineteenth-century innovation. Although New England's seventeenth-century Puritans were rarely as "puri-tanical" as they were later portrayed, the desire to impose a biblical mode of moral reform was part of their errand into the wilderness. Yet they largely pursued that mission within the small agricultural communities, originally numbering forty to fifty families, where the participants in the Great Migration of the 1630s settled. Nineteenth-century evangelicals operated in a very different cultural world. They inhabited an incipient era of mass culture, when the expansion of popular media and modes of transportation made the idea of national reform movements a true possibility. More important, they shared an enthusiasm for reform that was a product both of their own spiritual ambitions and the phenomena against which they were reacting.

The culmination of this release of spiritual energy was the creation of the "moral establishment" that characterized nineteenth-century America. The phrase covers a wide array of topics. It includes, for example, the fact that most states refused to extend the right to testify in court to individuals who did not believe in divine judgment in the world to come. It could still justify occasional prosecutions for blasphemy. These cases are so rare, so "aberrational," that their existence poses something of a puzzle. As Leonard Levy comments in his study of *Blasphemy*, "The number of prosecutions in the states was so few and the records so sparse that the prosecutions seem unlikely, inexplicable." They were instigated not to repress the open expression of heretical or atheistic thoughts, but rather to punish isolated individuals whose offensive musings had offended some upright (or uptight) citizen or official. In one of the two leading cases, *People v. Ruggles*[27] (1812), the blasphemous proclamation was likely part of a drunken rant. In the other leading case, *Commonwealth v. Kneeland*[28] (1832–1836), the provocation was more substantive: lectures and articles written by Abner Kneeland, "a cantankerous, inflexible heretic," Levy called him, who was "regarded as an immoral being who had crawled forth from some Stygian cave to menace Massachusetts." Ruggles and Kneeland hardly seem noteworthy culprits in the annals of heresy. Yet in the decisions affirming their guilt, two of the nation's preeminent jurists, Chancellor James Kent of New York and Chief Justice Leland Shaw of Massachusetts, upheld an orthodox conception of blasphemy.[29] The rationale for these decisions was not to defend Christianity per se, or to protect its doctrines against intellectual abuse, much less to imply that Christianity remained an established religion. The sustaining claim was rather that Christianity was the source of the moral convictions that informed American law and common law more generally. To preserve that moral fabric, certain core truths of Christianity deserved protection.[30]

There were, however, far more serious dangers to post-Revolutionary morality than the drunken comments or cantankerous rhetoric of isolated oddballs. As the evangelical reform agenda took shape in the early nineteenth century, three social evils appeared particularly alarming. One was the headlong proliferation of lotteries, legally chartered by the states to support any of a number of projects. The second was the massive increase in liquor consumption, in a nation veritably tippling its way to the pursuit of happiness, which led to the creation of *The Alcoholic Republic* that the historian William Rorabaugh has so aptly described, and which also made the argument for temperance so compelling.[31] The third was the desecration of the Sabbath through the application of the Jeffersonian principle that the closing of the post office on Sunday was an improper establishment of religion. The nineteenth-century post office was rarely a separate building; it was usually found in a store or tavern, and many American males were all too happy to favor a healthy libation or two over the hymns and the sermon.

The moral perfectionism of nineteenth-century evangelicals thus aspired to cure Americans of their undisciplined impulses to gamble, drink, and desecrate the injunctions of Exodus 20: 8–11. But this evangelical desire confronted serious constitutional obstacles. The desire to impose new legislative regulations on lotteries that continued to operate decades after they had been chartered ran afoul of the Supreme Court's deep respect for the vested rights of chartered corporations. Here the jurisprudence of the Contract Clause made it difficult to regulate lottery ventures that had yet to meet their targeted funding goals. In the realm of temperance, two other objections intervened. One was the belief that the sale and purchase of liquor were simple exercises of a personal right to property. The other was the concern that even if a state imposed some legal regime of temperance on its own residents, the Commerce Clause of Article I, Section 8 would still allow liquor to be imported from other states.

Antebellum legislators and judges certainly perceived the religious sentiments swirling through society, and evangelical reformers did enjoy some successes. But when their legislative victories were challenged in court, judges generally followed the standing legal doctrines that preferred the property rights of liquor and lottery vendors to the moral claims of reformers. These constitutional deterrents to political action had a powerful impact on evangelical reformers, leading them to adopt a more innovative approach to constitutional interpretation. They began developing arguments that would support a more democratic conception of the police power of states and localities to act broadly in support of public health and safety, as circumstances warranted. Evangelicals thus began moving toward the idea of a living Constitution that would empower decisive shifts in the moral beliefs of a democratic people to prevail over the doctrine of vested rights.[32]

The free expression of religion in antebellum America thus acquired an avowedly political character. Evangelical reformers founded countless societies to press their case, and these societies formed national alliances while relying on print media to disseminate their views. The idea of using shared moral concerns to unite denominations did mark a significant innovation in American democracy, akin to the organization of national political parties. Consistent with the ecumenicist impulse in American religiosity, this position allowed the competitors in the spiritual marketplace to disagree peacefully over the theological matters that Christians routinely debated but to cooperate politically on other social concerns that now united them. When Madison had imagined the beneficial effects of an argumentative Protestant culture, he was primarily concerned with the traditional issues of separation of church and state and the protection of conscience. The new agenda of social reform opened a different field of activity where tacit political alliances uniting members of different denominations coexisted with the multiplicity of sects Madison had invoked in *Federalist* 51.

There was, however, one subject of reform where the Madisonian model could never work. Temperance, lotteries, and Sabbatarianism were all issues that could be contended nationally; anti-slavery was not. Perhaps in the early nineteenth century, the focus on ending the Atlantic slave trade made some measure of national consensus conceivable. But the idea that Congress could also use its legislative power over interstate commerce to limit the *domestic* slave trade— a question that the Missouri Crisis of 1819–1820 exacerbated— proved deeply controversial. When outright abolitionism replaced the colonization of emancipated slaves as the true object of anti-slavery reform, the basis for unifying the great evangelical denominations collapsed. In the mid-1840s, Baptists and Methodists went their separate northern and southern ways, fracturing over the slavery issue, in the process confirming the gloomy reservation that Madison had nurtured all along. Back in 1787, he had told the Federal Convention that the great division among the states did not lie between large and small states, as the debate over representation falsely implied, "but principally from the effects of their having or not having slaves."[33] Three decades later, reflecting on the Missouri Crisis, he described the grave dangers the Union could face. "Should a state of parties arise, founded on geographical boundaries and other physical and permanent distinctions which happen to coincide with them, what is to control those great repulsive masses from awful shocks against each other?"[34] Christian charity and forbearance would never outweigh the respective commitments that South and North had made to slave and free labor.

The democratization of religion in the post-Revolutionary decades thus had overtly political implications that were just as important as its empowerment of the laity in church affairs. The free expression of religion now supported a broad agenda of public action. Moral reformers inspired by spiritual motives could beseech their fellow citizens and elected officials to apply religious values to public problems. If the law itself could not become a vehicle for advancing merely denominational interests, it had nevertheless become susceptible to values and sentiments grounded in consensual religious beliefs. That consensus was easier to form because individual denominations no longer feared that one of their competitors would gain an unfair advantage through its political power.

### BIBLE WARS AND AN IDEAL OF NEUTRALITY

Whether one calls it a "moral establishment" or an "indirect establishment," the idea that Christianity was an essential element of

American law and culture thus persisted in the post-Revolutionary decades. One noteworthy example of this lay in the restrictions many states retained on the right to give legal testimony. Those individuals who did not believe in the existence of a deity enforcing judgment in the world to come were deemed legally incompetent to testify. This restriction appeared acceptable because it imposed no burden on religious conscience, which remained free to believe whatever it wished to believe; it simply provided a prudent safeguard for the reliability of legal testimony.[35]

Yet the most important realm within which this moral establishment operated was public education. "The controversy over Protestant religious instruction in the nation's public schools and the public funding of religious/parochial schools," Steven Green has observed, "was arguably the most important church-state issue of the nineteenth century."[36] The belief that all citizens should be schooled marked one advanced salient in the American republican project. In Jefferson's revisal of the Virginia legal code, for example, bill 79, "for the More General Diffusion of Knowledge" ranked right along bill 82, "for Establishing Religious Freedom," as two paramount measures in his republican agenda. In Jefferson's enlightened view, children should be taught history first, religion later. They should, in effect, be given the critical tools needed to evaluate religious opinions, and thus to fulfill Locke's vision that one proper function of education was to promote an individual's ineluctable decision on matters of faith.

Most early supporters of public education did not share Jefferson's advanced views about the proper sequencing of historical and religious instruction. In their view, the Bible remained a universal source of human morality, and schoolchildren from an early age should be properly instructed in its profound truths. Instruction did *not* mean active interpretive commentary on the text, which could often reflect denominational preferences. That would come from

Sunday sermons, not weekday school lessons. But in a Protestant society imbued with the sacred principle of *sola Scriptura*, conventional wisdom readily accepted the idea that a direct if unmediated exposure to the Bible would give children essential moral tools. Children could learn the sublime teachings of Jesus without fretting about doctrinal nuance. This conviction shaped the ostensibly nonsectarian approaches of the Free School Society of New York City (founded in 1805) or the Massachusetts State Board of Education (which Horace Mann, the nation's best-known education reformer, led from 1836 to 1848).[37]

Yet this seemingly benign approach soon mustered its critics. Sectarian schools wondered why they should not be allowed to share the public funds that sustained the Free School Society. Evangelicals objected that the approach favored by Mann veered too close to the Unitarian convictions they fervently rejected. Catholics opposed the idea of an unmediated immersion in Scripture relying on the King James Bible. Those who believed that children should receive religious as well as moral or civic benefits from their introduction to Scripture remained wary of the minimalist goals of the nonsectarians. Nativists who were alarmed by the massive influx of Catholic immigrants in the 1830s felt that core Protestant values had to be reinforced against an autocratic, intolerant Roman church. By contrast, as nonsectarians grew more sensitive to the diversity of American religious beliefs that the processes of urbanization and immigration only enlarged, they struggled to develop another rationale for Bible reading that would avoid the religious tensions that sectarians fostered.

By the middle two decades of the century the "school controversy" had taken its mature, perhaps enduring form. A welter of claims defined the matrix of controversy, and it is the existence of this dispute, more than the articulation of a coherent doctrine, that best illustrates the complexities of American thought and practice.

On the one hand, the vitality of American religiosity presumed that children and citizens should know its dominant shared values. To read the Bible as a universal source of morality, to be given to students without any doctrinal inflection, identified an obvious method for inculcating essential values. If Catholics still balked at a Protestant approach to instruction, that only revealed their need for further Americanization. Because the mission of Bible reading was to present moral truth rather than religious doctrine, its defenders genuinely believed they were still conforming to the constitutional commitment to disestablishment.

Yet other participants in the controversy carried this commitment in a different direction—one more consistent with the animus shared by Jefferson and Madison. As the controversy moved from political bodies into the courts, judges arguably had to wrestle in a more principled way with the tension between moral improvement and constitutional liberty. In two early cases in Maine and Massachusetts, courts upheld the disciplining of Catholic students who balked at Bible readings on conscientious grounds, but they did so on grounds that emphasized the nonsectarian character of the activity. So long as teachers were not advancing explicitly religious doctrines, Catholic rights of conscience were not really being violated.

The nonsectarian approach thus opened a way to accommodate a residual religious commitment with the constitutional norm of disestablishment. But if one was troubled by this accommodation, or if one respected the conscience-based objections of Catholic students, the logic of the constitutional norm led to a more radical conclusion. That conclusion was reached in the Cincinnati-based case of *Board of Education v. Minor*,[38] "the most significant Bible reading case of the nineteenth century."[39] This "Bible wars" case drew national attention, and with its resolution by the Ohio Supreme Court in June 1873, the "school controversy" attained a new clarity.

In 1869 the Cincinnati school board adopted a new policy "prohibiting religious instruction" in the schools and eliminating Bible reading. Its primary motive was to persuade Catholic parents to send their children to public schools, rather than to pursue the dramatic expansion of enrollment in parochial schools. This decision in turn elicited a sharp reaction from much (though not all) of the Protestant clergy. Some critics of the policy held that the United States was indeed a Christian nation, and that this fact itself justified Bible reading. When the school board adhered to its policy, the protesters filed suit in the local superior court. Among other claims, the plaintiffs argued that the state constitution, echoing the Northwest Ordinance of 1787, positively obliged the legislature to promote "religion, morality and knowledge" among the citizens. Because Christianity was obviously the dominant religion in Ohio, its government remained free—or indeed bound—to disseminate its essential truths among students and citizens.

The superior court ruled 2–1 in favor of the plaintiffs, effectively suspending the school board's decision. The majority's two concurring opinions echoed Washington's Farewell Address (which the plaintiffs in fact cited): because "the moral sense" depended on "religious belief, estimated by a Christian standard," the state had a duty to convey essential religious truth to its children. In dissent, Judge Alphonso Taft (father of William Howard Taft) argued that Bible reading was an act of worship whose "use is a symbol of Protestant supremacy in the schools, and as such offensive to Catholics and to Jews." Government had to be neutral in its treatment of denominations and faiths, Taft argued. Nor could it allow the preferences of the majority of the community to provide the standard of behavior.[40] Religiosity was not determined by majority rule.

The Cincinnati school board quickly appealed the decision, but it took the Ohio Supreme Court a full three years to rule in favor of the school board's original policy. During this interval the national public debate continued. This debate did not produce a simple alignment. Instead, it generated a complex and fluid array of positions, ranging from evangelicals and nativists who wanted to enhance religious instruction in order to counteract Catholic influences to moderate and liberal Protestants who were sympathetic to Catholic objections and who worried about the dilution of the separation of church and state. Many Protestants still favored the unmediated reading of the Bible, while Jews and freethinkers preferred the complete elimination of anything resembling religious instruction or exercise.[41]

In its opinion, the Ohio Supreme Court could have ducked this charged debate and ruled on narrow grounds. Instead, Justice John Welch confronted the controversy directly, as a matter of first principles. In the opening section of his opinion, Welch held that the school board had acted well within its authority in its original decision. He rejected the contention that the state constitution's affirmation that "religion, morality, and knowledge" were all "essential to good government" constituted a positive command to provide religious instruction within the schools. The real meaning of this provision was that "*true* religion, *true* morality, and *true* knowledge shall be promoted, by encouraging schools and means of instruction," not by imposing a specific regime of religious and moral indoctrination, which the state legislature had never pretended to do.[42]

"This opinion might well end here," Welch then observed. But given the "peculiar importance" of the issue, he offered further reflections, "really lying outside of the case proper." What the critics of the school board really desired was the equation of religion with Christianity, which the authors of the Ohio constitution had rejected. "The true republican doctrine," Welch wrote, "is simple and easily understood. It means a free conflict of opinions as to things divine; and it means masterly inactivity on the part of the state, except for the purpose of keeping the conflict free, and preventing the violation of private rights or of the public peace." The government would support this process simply by supporting a system of education. "A man's right to his own religious convictions, and to impart them to his own children . . . are as sacred as his rights of person or property." The true object of the protection of religious freedom was to ensure the rights of the minority, because "The majority can protect itself." When objections existed to any mode of religious instruction, the proper solution was to number these subjects with all the others that "can more conveniently, satisfactorily, and safely be taught elsewhere."[43]

These "principles," Welch concluded, "are as old as Madison, and were his favorite opinions." Welch was right. He had studied Madison's published writings, which he quoted, and not for the mere rhetorical purpose of doing "law office history." Perhaps, had the population of Cincinnati (or Ohio) been more homogeneous and less disputatious, some other solution to the school controversy would have appeared. But the simple fact of the controversy demonstrated why government should not act. The true republican doctrine was what Madison had prescribed: remove government from an enterprise it had no capacity to supervise or direct, make the free exercise of religion as private an activity as possible, and remember that the great objective of protecting religion was to secure the minority against the majority, and not to enforce the majority's false claims to authority.

The significance of *Board of Education v. Minor* was *not* that it provided a happy consensual solution to an issue that some American communities still debate today. That outcome it clearly did not achieve. Catholics and many Protestants still thought that the banishment of Bible reading would impair the moral improvement of students. But where nonsectarian Bible reading still persisted, usually reduced to a few verses of text lacking any commentary, its justification grew increasingly secular in nature. The diversity in religious belief guaranteed by the commitment to free exercise made any overtly religious presentation impossible, except perhaps in small communities where one denomination dominated. Second, the eloquence of Justice Welch's opinion, which was more a matter of stating general principles than advancing legal doctrine, demonstrated the lasting legacy of Madison's and Jefferson's views. Welch shared Madison's optimistic view that "Time has at length revealed the true remedy" in "the American Theatre." The free competition of religious ideas and opinions in the United States revealed "the golden truth which it has taken the world eighteen centuries to learn, and which has at last solved the terrible enigma of 'church and state.'"[44] This was another form of revelation than the one given in Torah, the Gospel, and the Koran, but it was no less illuminating. Keeping faith with the wisdom of Madison and Jefferson had its own virtues because it articulated a civic vision that many Americans still admired.

## THE MOST AMERICAN RELIGION OF ALL

There was, however, one other religious revelation that had a critical impact on "the terrible enigma of 'church and state.'" Whether one treats Joseph Smith as the true prophet of a new dispensation revealed in the Book of Mormon or the greatest con man of nineteenth-century American culture, the creation of the Church of Jesus Christ of Latter Day Saints (LDS) after 1830 marked the most innovative enterprise in American religious history. As Gordon Word has argued, Mormonism is the most American religion of all, not merely for its audacious act of theological creation (or discovery), but also for the complex way in which its doctrines synthesized so many aspects of American culture. Mormonism was, Wood writes, "both mystical and secular; communitarian and individualistic; hierarchical and congregational; authoritarian and democratic; antinomian and Arminian; anti-clerical and priestly; revelatory and empirical; utopian and practical; ecumenical and nationalist."[45] Proclaiming the discovery of an ancient Scripture supplementing the Old and New Testaments, Joseph Smith consciously became a prophet in the full meaning of the term. Where Christians readily dismissed the Book of Mormon as a sacrilegious appendix to the biblical canon, the Prophet and his acolytes held that it confirmed the continuing activity of a global god who could convey revelations to later generations just as he had done to the prophets of the ancient Levant.[46] This conviction empowered Mormons to claim that their new dispensation superseded the authority of other denominations. They balked at accepting the pluralism of American religiosity. "Like Catholics, Mormons operated with the formal assumption that theirs was the one, true, and universal church," Chris Beneke observes, rejecting the common belief that a general acceptance of the core elements of Christianity united other denominations even when they disagreed over so many other issues.[47]

The religious violence that Mormons suffered—including the Prophet's murder in Carthage, Illinois, on June 27, 1844—has no parallel in American history. Although the Mormon persecution is a pale reflection of the massacres and martyrdoms that racked Reformation Europe, it marked a radical departure from the conditions that had governed American Christendom. Some of that animus reflected the belief that the ostensible discovery of the Golden Plates that Joseph Smith deciphered with the magical aid of seer stones was simply a hoax to disguise the blasphemous fiction that the Book of Mormon perpetrated. Because there was no effective way to prosecute blasphemy in the United States, anti-Mormon prejudice took a different form. Mormon doctrine could not be suppressed, but could Mormon behavior be regulated? Mormon migrants who were "initially welcomed" as industrious pioneers in Ohio, Missouri, and

Illinois soon sparked a militant resistance that transcended qualms about the textual authenticity of the Book of Mormon. Two claims seemed paramount. One was the Mormons' desire to create legally autonomous communities of their own, in which the bonds connecting church and state would be restored, not severed. The other was the growing suspicion that Mormon leaders were becoming active polygamists. That practice began at a relatively early point. The Revelation of Celestial Marriage that Smith received in 1843 made polygamy a defining element of Mormon culture. But even then the church did its best to keep the practice a secret, until Smith's successor Brigham Young announced it to the public in 1852, five years after he led the epic hegira to the Great Salt Lake Basin.[48]

When their advance parties arrived in 1847, that desolate country was still under Mexican jurisdiction. The Treaty of Guadalupe Hidalgo soon transferred that authority to the United States. The church quickly sought admission to the Union as the state of Deseret, but Congress instead organized the Mormon settlement as the territory of Utah. Under Article IV, Section 3 of the Constitution, that left the territorial government and the future question of statehood under congressional supervision. Still, Utah was a distant land, settled by migrants unified in their faith, and led by a highly disciplined church. The territorial legislature was an extension of the LDS church, and it quickly adopted measures that enhanced its authority. The LDS church was legally incorporated, but without the marked limitations on property holding found in other states. Where other states treated marriage as a nonsacramental legal contract, in Utah the church enjoyed full legal authority over the institution. Far from shielding polygamy as a legal secret, Mormon leaders could celebrate its advantages and treat it as one of the great accomplishments of their New Dispensation.[49]

The open celebration of this remarkable innovation after 1852 became the great fault line of conflict between Mormon Utah and the rest of American culture. If Mormons were one more outgrowth of the Second Great Awakening, their marital practices deeply offended the convictions of the evangelical community and Americans more generally. Women bound to the yoke of plural marriage could not be viewed as individuals freely expressing their religious conscience. Their husbands had to be avatars of unbridled sexual license, rather than patriarchs bearing the difficult task of managing their complex households. Companionate marriage between two consenting adults was the moral norm that Mormons wantonly violated. Along with slavery, plural marriage now ranked as one of the "twin relics of barbarism" that northern public opinion openly reprobated.

Had "the Principle" been revealed to Mormon leaders *after* the putative state of Deseret had been admitted to the Union, the American conception of the free exercise of religion might have evolved along a different trajectory. Basic principles of federalism devolved the primary responsibility for regulating religion to the states. Mormons hoped that the existing norms of experimental religion left them ample room for innovation. Even if the tacit establishment that the LDS secured in Utah deviated from the dominant norm prevailing elsewhere, their isolation in the remote Great Basin could have allowed their state to become the lone exception that proved the general rule of disestablishment.

Alas, this intriguing counterfactual story remains untold. Congress retained its residual jurisdiction over the territory. In 1862, with states'-rights Democrats absent from Congress, the Morrill Act adopted by strong Republican majorities made bigamy illegal in the territories, under criminal penalty; stripped the LDS of its corporate status; and restricted the value of real estate any religious society could own to $50,000. As Gordon notes, the Morrill Act was also the equivalent of a "second disestablishment," and thus akin to the work done to unpack the moral establishment created after 1789—except that now it was the mainstream Protestant belief in the sanctity of Christian marriage that was assaulting the experimental audacity of the Mormons.[50] This view treated the plural wives of Mormon households as an exploited group, and the legal and political challenge that the federal government faced was to crack the hegemony of a male patriarchy. Statehood and autonomy were the prizes the LDS church could gain by conforming to the Morrill Act, but only if the church abolished the Principle or left it to cope on isolated ranches in distant canyons beyond effective scrutiny.

Mormons instead pursued a "legally sophisticated" strategy of resistance, not surrender. Acting within the fervor of their profound convictions, they argued that the attack on the Principle was a betrayal of the nation's commitment to religious liberty. Even though only a minority of Mormon households practiced it, plural marriage was a controlling element of their faith, a goal that all scrupulous Mormons should strive to fulfill, and indeed a foundation of their attack on American culture with its corrupting reliance on monogamy.[51] Notwithstanding their aggressive denunciations of the Protestant culture they believed they had superseded, Mormons still hoped their bid for statehood would prevail. After Congress refused their applications, Mormons became more interested in securing a judicial solution to their dilemma, in part to protect their prominent leaders who remained subject to criminal prosecution under the Morrill Act. In 1874 Congress adopted the Poland Act, which broadened federal jurisdiction within Utah at the expense of Mormon-dominated territorial courts. Equally important, the Poland Act allowed polygamy convictions to be appealed to the Supreme Court.

The basis for a test case of the Morrill Act was thus laid, and the youthful George Reynolds, having newly taken a second wife, became the named defendant. As his trial neared, the defense strategy shifted from seeking an outright verdict to denying the court any evidence that a second marriage had occurred. That gambit of "obfuscation" failed when the "uncoached" but "visibly pregnant" second wife was summoned to testify. Her testimony proved that polygamy had occurred, and after a retrial reached the same verdict, an appeal to the Supreme Court was readied.[52]

Like the Bible wars, *Reynolds v. U.S.* commanded national attention. Attorney General Charles Devens made the case for the government; the Mormons turned to the much younger but still distinguished George Washington Biddle. There was a powerful asymmetry between their arguments. Biddle pursued a more overtly constitutional path. True, he placed some reliance on *Dred Scott v. Sandford*[53]—already the most reviled decision in American constitutional law, as it has ever remained—because it had imposed limits on congressional authority over territorial law. Biddle relied on the traditional understanding of American federalism that had survived the Civil War, and which the Supreme Court's approach to the Fourteenth Amendment was also reinforcing. The law of marriage remained a subject of state (or territorial) law with which Congress could not interfere. Arguing the other side, Devens drew upon the denunciations of polygamy that had become so prevalent over the past quarter-century.[54]

The case was argued in mid-November 1878 and resolved two months later, when a unanimous court upheld Reynolds's conviction. Chief Justice Morrison Waite's opinion took a decidedly historical turn, and it largely ignored the jurisdictional claims of the Mormons. The real question was not whether Congress had the authority to legislate for the territories; it simply involved "the guilt of one who knowingly violates a law which has been properly enacted if he entertains a religious belief that the law is wrong." Did the congressional prohibition on polygamy violate Reynolds's free exercise of religion under the First Amendment? One could answer that question only by examining the meaning of "the word 'religion,'" and the best way to do that was to turn "to the history of the times in the midst of which the provision was adopted. The precise point of the inquiry is what is the religious freedom which has been guaranteed."[55]

Much like Justice Welch in Ohio, Chief Justice Waite turned readily to the prestigious authority of Jefferson and Madison. Extracting key sentences from their seminal documents, Waite quickly reached a simple but strong conclusion. "Congress was deprived of all legislative power over mere opinion, but was left free to reach actions which were in violation of social duties or subversive of good order." Polygamy was a criminal act in English and American law, subject even to capital punishment. Nor was there any doubt that its association with antique forms of patriarchy would be destructive of a republican social order. "Laws are made for the government of actions," Waite concluded, "and while they cannot interfere with mere religious belief and opinions, they may with practices." Mormons had a moral right to believe in the revelation of the Principle, but if they willingly practiced it, as George Reynolds had, they were subject to legal constraints and penalties.

One could fault Waite's opinion for its brevity and its casual anointment of Madison and Jefferson as the preeminent authorities on the separation of church and state. By modern standards, *Reynolds v. U.S.* is a very concise opinion, given the import of its holding. More could have been expected from the Court's first decision on free exercise. Yet given the radical disjunction between Mormon practice and customary beliefs about marriage, the opinion went as far as it had to go. There was no real need to articulate a robust doctrine of free exercise, replete with qualifications, distinctions, or levels of scrutiny. "To permit this would be to make the professed doctrines of religious belief superior to the law of the land, and, in effect, to permit every citizen to become a law unto himself," Waite wrote. "Government could exist only in name under such circumstances."[56] This affirmation of a basic principle and a binary distinction between belief and behavior did all the necessary work. Nor was Waite mangling the historical record by invoking Jefferson and Madison. Their notions of free exercise were not framed to ask when individuals could use religion to seek exemptions from duly enacted laws governing ordinary behavior. They were instead conceived and deployed to guard a realm of private religious choice about matters of faith and worship. The full articulation of a doctrine of religious liberty had to await the further expansion of the regulatory power of American governance and the appearance of other faiths and sects—notably the Jehovah's Witnesses—armed with their own zealous visions of religious freedom.

## CHAPTER FIVE

# An Era of Doctrines

*BOARD OF EDUCATION of Cincinnati v. Minor*[1] and *Reynolds v. United States*,[2] the two great cases in nineteenth-century American religious jurisprudence, were more matters of principle than statements of legal doctrine. *Minor* held that any effort to teach children essential religious truths based on majority opinions would violate the legitimate rights of the minority. *Reynolds* involved a simple distinction between belief and behavior. Neither case required courts to elaborate a legal *doctrine* of religious freedom—to develop a set of qualified rules and tests to allow interpreters to distinguish different kinds of challenges and remedies that require or prohibit some action by the state. The existence of such a doctrine presupposes that religious claims of various kinds will work their way into court, and as cases multiply and grow more complex, a framework will emerge to manage these claims in a coherent way.

The task of developing a doctrine of religious freedom began circa 1940, with Jehovah's Witnesses acting as a catalytic force bringing one case after another to the Supreme Court. The results of the formulation of this doctrine have not been entirely happy. This area of law remains so contested that any knowing commentator would warn readers not to suppose that any truly coherent doctrine actually exists. Instead we have a staggering set of disputes and sites of disagreement. Kent Greenawalt's learned survey of contemporary free exercise topics, for example, comprises twenty-two chapters and a conclusion. Each chapter covers multiple issues, and Greenawalt assumes that a successful account of free exercise jurisprudence requires a nuanced analysis fraught with many distinctions of values and circumstances.[3]

Historians have no capacity to resolve these disputes by appealing to the evidence of the past. The best they can do is to recover the context within which these disputes originated and to identify some of the historical connections, complexities, and ironies that bedevil this realm of jurisprudence. The analysis of a judicial doctrine by legal scholars will take a different path. Such an analysis is inherently *endogenous* in nature. It emphasizes the content and connections of relevant decisions, opinions, and enactments; identifies the problems and tensions that these texts leave open; and then considers how the law should evolve to resolve those difficulties. Historical analysis, by contrast, is inherently *exogenous*. Though mindful of the content of opinions and statutes, its real concerns lie with the intentions, ambitions, and strategies of the actors: the litigants, the lawyers who represent and often select them, the jurists who hear their cases, the politicians who support and oppose their causes. Historians cannot really weigh the merits of particular decisions; they would find it difficult or even pointless to ask whether a case was rightly decided, a question that legal scholars weigh routinely. But the origins and consequences of particular decisions and acts are another issue entirely.

Any survey of modern free exercise doctrine would have to round up the usual set of leading cases. At the very least, this survey would include these decisions and acts:

- the antecedent case of *Pierce v. Society of Sisters* (1923),[4] in which a unanimous Supreme Court voided an Oregon statute requiring parents to send their children to public schools and therefore allowed them to determine for themselves how their children would be educated intellectually and religiously;
- the cluster of cases (1938–1946) in which Jehovah's Witnesses sought legal protection from the various forms of persecution to which they were subjected;[5]
- *Sherbert v. Verner* (1963),[6] which involved a Seventh Day Adventist seeking unemployment compensation after refusing to work on Saturday;
- *Wisconsin v. Yoder* (1971),[7] in which the Court allowed Amish parents to withdraw their children from public school at age fourteen, although the state required attendance until age sixteen;
- *Oregon Employment Division v. Smith* (1990),[8] a.k.a. the peyote case, in which the Supreme Court declined to grant faith-based exemptions to neutral, general-purpose statutes enacted without any animus against religious beliefs or practices;
- the federal Religious Freedom Restoration Act (1993), commonly known as RFRA, adopted in response to the criticisms of *Oregon Employment Division v. Smith* made by numerous religious groups, which sought to restore as a federal legislative matter the general understanding of accommodations permitted under *Sherbert v. Verner* and *Wisconsin v. Yoder*;
- *City of Boerne v. Flores* (1997),[9] a case involving a local zoning restriction on the expansion of a Texas church, in which the Court held that Congress was not empowered to impose RFRA on state and local governments;

- the congressional response to *City of Boerne* in the Religious Land Use and Institutionalized Persons Act (2000), commonly known as RLUIPA; and
- *Hobby Lobby v. Burwell* (2014),[10] in which a narrowly divided Supreme Court allowed a private corporation owned by a religiously scrupulous family to assert a free exercise right against funding certain contraceptive procedures covered by the Affordable Care Act of 2010.

This list of cases is hardly comprehensive; any qualified professor of constitutional law could easily identify other noteworthy decisions, such as *Church of the Lukumi Babalu Aye, Inc., v. Hialeah* (1993),[11] which concerned a municipal ordinance consciously designed to prevent the ritual slaughter of chickens by Santerians; *Gonzalez v. O Centro Espírita Beneficente União do Vegetal* (2006),[12] which involved the drinking of a hallucinogenic tea (*hoasca*) popular along the Amazon—a fact situation very similar to the peyote case; or *Masterpiece Cakeshop v. Colorado* (2018),[13] which stemmed from a baker's religiously scrupulous refusal to sell a wedding cake to a same-sex couple. Another continuously important realm of jurisprudence pivots on the requests of incarcerated prisoners' to be able to practice their religion freely.[14]

What can historians add to a barebones summary of the constitutional doctrine of the free exercise of religion? Clarifying its complexities, controversies, and confusions lies far beyond their competence. But viewing these decisions and difficulties from the perspective of history may still have some advantages on particular issues. Perhaps, too, there is something to be said for restating the underlying genius of the approach that Jefferson and Madison pioneered, with its emphasis on doing as much as possible to treat religion as a wholly private matter.

After sketching the emergence of modern free exercise doctrine, then, this concluding chapter will offer a set of historically grounded comments on modern controversies. Historians in general are more comfortable talking about *legacies* rather than *lessons*, or consequences rather than applications, but in this realm of inquiry it is possible that both modes of viewing the past still apply. The founding generation certainly believed it could draw manifest lessons from the history of religious persecution, and if Jefferson and Madison believed that the application of those lessons had brought happy results, the least we owe them is to consider the basis of their beliefs.

## THE WITNESSES' LEGAL CRUSADE

On October 22, 1935, ten-year-old Billy Gobitas[15] refused to salute the American flag during the daily patriotic ritual at his Minersville, Pennsylvania school. His teacher tried to drag Billy's right arm into the extended position that was then the style of the flag salute, but Billy grabbed his pocket with the tightest fist he could make. The next day his twelve-year-old sister Lilian followed his example. Billy and Lilian had already discussed this with their parents, Walter and Ruth, the owners of a small grocery. Walter was the Catholic son of Lithuanian immigrants; Ruth was a Methodist by birth. Their marriage was itself a mark of American toleration. But Ruth's parents had become Bible Students, a fundamentalist and evangelical sect that soon rechristened itself Jehovah's Witnesses, and in 1931 Ruth and Walter joined their church, too.[16]

Like most Witnesses, the Gobitases were truly devout, and Lilian and Billy had already gone out ringing doorbells to distribute the sect's literature. Their schoolhouse protest was their own decision, prompted by learning about a Witness third-grader in Massachusetts who had been expelled for refusing to salute the flag. They knew that Joseph Rutherford, the sect's autocratic leader, had associated the American salute with the Nazi salute in Germany, where Bible Students were suffering severe discrimination. But the children's opposition ultimately rested on the Ten Commandments. "Thou shalt not make unto thee any graven image, nor bow down to them nor serve them," Billy quoted Exodus XX in the letter he wrote the school district on November 5, 1935, "for the Lord thy God am a jealous God visiting the iniquity of the father upon the children unto the third and fourth generation of them that hate me."[17]

The school district could have allowed Billy and Lilian to stand quietly as their schoolmates pledged the flag. But Superintendent Charles Roudabush held strong beliefs, too. Though personally fond of the Gobitases, he found their sectarian rigor unsettling. The result was litigation. A decade earlier, in *Gitlow v. New York*,[18] the Supreme Court held that some of the clauses enumerated in the federal Bill of Rights—beginning with freedom of speech and press—applied to regulation by state and local governments. The case that the Gobitases now filed sought to extend that principle to the free exercise of religion. *Gobitis* (as it is misspelled) *v. Minersville School District*[19] represented a turning point in the massive litigation campaign that Hayden Covington, the sect's lead attorney, waged in the late 1930s and early 1940s. There were dozens of such cases, generated by the fervor of the Witnesses, the zeal with which they denounced the corruptions of every other Christian denomination, and the numerous and often brutal instances of repression they encountered across the country.

Both the federal district court and a three-judge panel of the Court of Appeals for the Third Circuit ruled for the family, citing the Free Exercise clause and the Due Process clause of the Fourteenth Amendment to hold that sincere acts of conscience trumped any plausible basis for denying the children access to school. Even so, the Minersville school district pursued its appeal. On March 4, 1940, the Supreme Court granted certiorari. Oral argument occurred seven weeks later, and the Court handed down a unanimous ruling, reversing the decision and upholding the school district, on June 3, 1940.

An ocean away, the British army was ending its retreat from Dunkirk, leaving the Low Countries and northern France under *Wehrmacht* occupation. That distant fact sustained the deeper rationale behind the decision. In the Court's internal deliberations, Chief Justice Charles Evans Hughes first endorsed the school district's position. The next five justices deferred commenting; then it was Felix Frankfurter's turn to speak. Frankfurter delivered an impassioned statement defending the school ceremony as an essential means of fostering national patriotism. Many of the former Harvard law professor's long-winded remarks drove his judicial brethren to distraction. But this one was well received, and once the justices voted on the case, Hughes asked Frankfurter to draft the opinion.[20]

Like President Franklin Roosevelt, whom he often consulted, Frankfurter assumed that American entrance in the war would be needed to overcome Nazi hegemony in Europe, and as an active if nonobservant member of the Jewish community, the Vienna-born immigrant understood the catastrophic consequences of a German triumph. Freedom of conscience was important. But no one was preventing the Witnesses from maintaining their beliefs. Their children were simply being asked to perform a ritual promoting the civic solidarity all Americans should share. His opinion was an ode to patriotism and national unity, coupled with a strong affirmation that courts were incompetent to substitute their preferences for legislative judgment. The use of education to promote compliance with a uniform set of civic values, Frankfurter concluded, "may be utilized so long as men's right to believe as they please, to win others to their way of belief, and their right to assemble in their chosen places of worship for the devotional ceremonies of their faith, are all fully respected."[21]

This position slighted the critical exception that Justice Harlan Fiske Stone, the sole dissenter in *Gobitis*, had promulgated in the now-famous Footnote 4 to the Court's recent decision in *Carolene Products v. U.S.* (1938).[22] There Stone had intimated that while the Court would henceforth adopt what we call a "reasonable basis" for assessing the validity of economic legislation, it could still apply more rigorous standards of review when legislative acts impaired the rights of "discrete and insular minorities" who could not gain redress for their grievances through ordinary politics. That was a standard that the Witnesses—like African Americans in the Jim Crow South— could easily meet. No denomination since the Mormons had worked harder to offend other churches. But where the Mormons found refuge in their Utah exile, Jehovah's Witnesses were scattered across numerous communities where their carping against other churches was not taken lightly.[23]

Hearing that Frankfurter would read his opinion from the bench, Stone decided to do the same with his dissent, and he did so even after Frankfurter read only the usual succinct summary of the case and decision. There was no reason to suspect the Gobitas family of any disloyalty to the United States, Stone declared. All they sought was to avoid complying with an action "which violates their deep-est religious convictions." The constitutional protection of acts of conscience made some "reasonable accommodation" between the interests of government and the liberty of the individual essential. In this instance, where the evidence of harm to the republic seemed so hazy, the Constitution "command[ed] that freedom of mind and spirit must be preserved."[24]

Stone soon discovered that his act of judicial conscience was far more valued both within the legal community and the press than Frankfurter's opinion. Yet the Court had spoken. Its judgment that a communal power to demand patriotic observances of its population outweighed the conscience claims of individual dissenters was now the law of the land. The immediate result, however, was less an upsurge of patriotic feeling than a signal that it was open season for the legal coercion and social harassment of Jehovah's Witnesses. Intimidation came in countless forms, from municipal efforts to prevent Witnesses from distributing their literature or haranguing passersby to beatings, burnings, and other situations that left many adherents terrified for their lives. To the numerous suits Hayden Covington and other attorneys had already filed, these incidents soon generated a fresh wave of complaints. Whatever respect the Witnesses owed the Court—and their legal campaign assumed that the Court could be brought to their side—they owed a deeper obligation to the teachings of their faith.

Other than Frankfurter, members of the Court were nervous about their decision, and the editorial reactions that *Gobitis* provoked sharpened their concern. Nor was the administration entirely happy with this outcome. As the nation moved closer to war in 1940–1941, the New Dealers consciously portrayed the struggle against European fascism and Japanese militarism as a war between democratic values and the brutal oppression that the Axis powers imposed on their own citizens and the nations they occupied. At the heart of the New Deal's approach lay the conviction that the rights Americans enjoyed were not limited to traditional common-law procedures, but could be expressed more broadly in an emerging language of human rights inspired in part by President Roosevelt's four freedoms: freedom of expression and religion, the core values of the First Amendment, coupled with freedom from want and fear.[25]

That viewpoint was shared by two new appointments to the Court that Roosevelt made after *Gobitis* was decided: the veteran New Deal lawyer and former Solicitor and Attorney General, Robert Jackson, and Judge Wiley Rutledge of the Court of Appeals for the

DC Circuit, who publicly criticized the ruling in a commencement address at the University of Colorado.[26] Two Department of Justice lawyers, acting with the approval of Attorney General Francis Biddle, also published a quasi-official article urging the Court to reconsider *Gobitis*.[27] As the persecution of the Witnesses continued, the justices knew that the case needed revisiting.

The occasion came in 1943, with *West Virginia State Board of Education v. Barnette*, a case identical in every fact that mattered with *Gobitis* (including misspelling the lead plaintiff's name, which was Barnett). As in *Gobitis*, a federal district court panel had ruled for the schoolchildren. But now the judge writing the opinion, John Parker, sided with Stone's dissent in *Gobitis*. The appeal went directly to the Supreme Court, which had recently favored the Witnesses in several other cases. Once *Barnette* was argued, now Chief Justice Stone—the lone dissenter in *Gobitis*—assigned the opinion to Jackson, perhaps to ensure that he stuck with the majority. Tactically, this was a wise move when the Court was about to reverse a recent decision. But it also meant that Jackson might draft the opinion on narrower grounds than his brethren would have preferred. The former attorney general felt little sympathy for the Witnesses. Jackson openly doubted that their obnoxious version of free exercise was what the Constitution meant to protect.

The Court in *Barnette* voted 6–3 to overrule *Gobitis*. Jackson turned the opinion away from a broad reliance on the claim the Witnesses valued most: that the children's refusal to pledge allegiance was a fair exercise of their religious freedom. The question did not "turn on one's possession of particular religious views or the sincerity with which they are held," Jackson wrote. Other citizens lacking this religious motive could similarly oppose this "compulsory rite to infringe constitutional liberty of the individual." Jackson instead stressed the inadequacy of the legislative authority of the state to compel citizens to perform the salute.

Jackson linked the right not to perform the salute with the "clear and present danger" free speech doctrine that the Court had begun fashioning two decades earlier. Originally, the invocation of clear and present danger had complemented the open-ended "bad tendency" test that gave public authorities ample room to regulate public speech. But in a series of dissents and concurrences, Justices Oliver Wendell Holmes Jr. and Louis Brandeis had turned clear and present danger into a much tougher standard, effectively broadening the scope of constitutionally protected political speech. In the case of the Witness children, Justice Jackson reasoned that refusing to perform a brief innocuous ceremony obviously posed no clear and present danger to public welfare or security.[28]

Numerous questions have arisen over the substance and doctrinal details of this major shift in the jurisprudence of freedom of speech. That controversy need not concern us here. Yet one significant question remains, and the two concurring opinions in the *Barnette* case indicate why. What was the most appropriate basis for justifying the silent protests of the children? Why did the Free Exercise Clause not provide a sufficient basis for their refusal to salute the flag? Why did the Court instead rely on general notions of freedom of speech, with claims of conscience appearing only tangentially?

On these points the *Barnette* majority did not reach a complete consensus. In their concurrence, Justices Hugo Black and William O. Douglas recognized the "devoutness" of the children's beliefs, as measured "by their willingness to suffer persecution and punishment." Such beliefs did not immunize conscientious individuals from their general obligations to obey "laws which are . . . imperatively necessary to protect society as a whole from grave and pressingly imminent dangers." But in weighing such claims, the Court had to ask what ends were secured by "compelling little children to participate in a ceremony which ends in nothing for them but a fear of spiritual condemnation." If the children's "fears are groundless,"

the two justices suggested, "time and reason are the proper anti-
dotes for their errors." A pledge extracted from citizens out of fear
of coercion was "inconsistent with our Constitution's plan and purpose." This appeal to "time and reason" echoed Jefferson's justificatory preamble to the Virginia Statute for Religious Freedom. Justice
Frank Murphy's additional concurrence in *Barnette* made that link
more explicit by quoting Jefferson's "trenchant" and "unanswer-
able" language: "all attempts to influence [the mind] by temporal
punishments, or burdens, or by civil incapacitations, tend only to
beget habits of hypocrisy and meanness."[29]

The great puzzle of the Flag Salute cases pivots not on explaining the reversal in *Barnette* but in justifying the initial error in *Gobitis*.
That decision was widely criticized from the outset, and indeed
the three concurring justices in *Barnette* had felt misgivings almost
immediately. Perhaps the best one can say of Frankfurter's logic is
that it marked an early demonstration of judicial restraint, a confession that courts should not act as arbiters of decisions communities
could make for themselves. No one was asking the Gobitas children
to abandon their beliefs; all the school board wanted was to have
them engage in an activity supporting the patriotic ethos on which
the protection of American liberties ultimately depended. Even so,
*Gobitis* remains an anomalously strained decision that one struggles
to defend.[30]

There is another sense in which the Flag Salute cases echoed
issues that had long agitated American Protestants. Refusing to
pledge allegiance to the flag was politically akin to declining to swear
a legal oath as a violation of the fourth commandment against taking
the Lord's name in vain. Indeed, in a moral sense it was equivalent to
the public confession of conversion that was so essential an element
of American Protestantism. Unlike the Mormon practice of plural
marriage, the behavioral consequences of this act were slight, but in
the realm of conscience its implications ran deep. The question of

whether children should salute the flag was a political counterpart to the "indifferent" matters that had vexed seventeenth-century English Protestants. Which constitutional principle or legal act could possibly justify repression for a symbolic act?

Yet whether they were balking at pledging the flag or politely ⁣⁣⁣⁣⁣⁣⁣⁣⁣⁣⁣⁣⁣⁣⁣⁣⁣⁣⁣⁣⁣⁣⁣⁣⁣⁣ Witness performances were symbolic — or at least inoffensive—in a way that their adult brethren often were not. By contrast, the opposition to conscription that sent over four thousand adult Witnesses to jail during World War II marked an overt defiance of the law that could never gain public sympathy.[31] Their public behavior was offensive, and the insults they slathered on other religions rivaled the contumacy of seventeenth-century Quakers. Because Witnesses were so eager to make public protestations of their zeal, they disputed the authority of any official who sought to regulate their vocal performances or the public distribution of their printed materials.

In a subset of their numerous legal challenges, the Witnesses led the Supreme Court to develop new criteria for regulating controversial public speech. In *Cantwell v. Connecticut*,[32] the Supreme Court overturned the convictions of Nelson Cantwell, a "special pioneer" of the Witnesses' Watch Tower Society, and his two sons. The Cantwells had been leading an itinerant, proselytizing life that plunged them into poverty without shaking any of their spiritual ambitions. In April 1938 they were working a heavily Catholic neighborhood in New Haven, happily denouncing the Church of Rome at every corner and doorstep. When one homeowner complained to the police, the Cantwells were arrested for failing to obtain a license allowing them to solicit donations and for breaching the peace by playing an "offensive" record to persons on the street. A unanimous Court ruled that the statute authorizing officials to determine whether the Witnesses needed to obtain a license before seeking donations violated the Religion Clause by allowing the state to engage in a "censorship of religion as a means of determining its right to survive." The crucial factor was that the state was exercising the authority to determine "whether the cause is a religious one" or not, making the state a judge of religious activity. Even if the state permitted judicial remedies after a license was denied, it would still be engaging in "previous restraint," which the American doctrine of freedom of speech and press deemed "inadmissible."[33] Authorities remained free to punish fraudulent acts and to determine when solicitations could take place. The Cantwells had no legal right to crank up their portable record player at 3 a.m. to summon slumbering Catholics to hear their church's failings, but the state could not constitutionally prosecute Jesse Cantwell, the son charged with breaching the peace by playing the offensive record to two passersby. Even if his actions annoyed his listeners, they did not create a clear and present danger of violence.

*Cantwell* marked an important step not only in the incorporation of the Free Exercise Clause under the Fourteenth Amendment but also in providing a modern definition of the free exercise of religion. Free expression included the right to preach in public, to approach strangers, and even (at least briefly) to belabor them with spiritual opinions they might find offensive. A week after the oral argument in *Cantwell*, another incident in Rochester, New Hampshire, led to a case that marked an outer limit for offensive speech.

Walter Chaplinsky was the son of a Pennsylvania coal miner. In the early 1930s, when he was in his late teens, his family joined the Witnesses. Walter was soon a zealous missionary in the cause, eventually taking an assignment to proselytize in New Hampshire. In 1939 and 1940, numerous Witnesses there were arrested for preaching and soliciting without a license; Walter spent forty "brutal" days in jail after one such arrest. On April 6, 1940, he set up spiritual shop in the Rochester town square, and quickly drew a hostile crowd. When the city marshal came to monitor the disturbance, he urged

Walter to tone down his remarks, to no avail. Chaplinsky also refused
to salute the American flag. Rather than guard Chaplinsky from the
irate crowd or urge them to disperse, the marshal left the Witness
to be beaten. Eventually several policemen manhandled him back
to their station, ostensibly for his protection, while wholly ignoring
his tormentors. Outraged by his mistreatment, Chaplinsky snapped
back that the marshal was "a damn fascist and a racketeer," echoing
remarks he had made back in the town square.[34]

Remarks like these formed the basis for the "fighting words"
doctrine spawned by *Chaplinsky v. New Hampshire*.[35] The Supreme
Court unanimously upheld Chaplinsky's conviction for the public
use of "offensive, derisive, or annoying speech," which the state
court had limited to "words likely to cause the average addressee"
to fight. Had the Court wanted to err on the side of protecting religious freedom, it easily could have ruled otherwise. Verbal abuse had
flown both ways in the town square, and the police could have been
faulted for losing control of the situation. Instead their exhaustion
and their confessed disgust with the Witnesses prevailed. But writing for the Court, Justice Murphy—usually the Witnesses' leading
supporter—categorized "the 'fighting' words" directed against the
policemen as "utterances" that added nothing to "any exposition of
ideas," and which therefore merited no legal protection.[36]

Notwithstanding the religious zeal that colored this whole episode, legal scholars regularly treat *Chaplinsky* as a free speech rather
than a free exercise case. Yet the circumstances of the case effectively replicated the conditions that accompanied the evolution of
tolerationist ideas in the sixteenth and seventeenth centuries. In
their inner zeal and vituperative enthusiasm, Jehovah's Witnesses
in the 1930s and 1940s were direct descendants of the Anabaptists,
Quakers, Ranters, and other dissenters who gave the Reformation
its vitriolic edge. They embodied the evils of that most dangerous
human organ, the tongue, that source of offensive incivility that had

plagued theological controversies and the daily intercourse of ordinary believers.[37]

Yet in the United States—decidedly unlike Nazi Germany—the Witnesses inhabited a world where the ambit of free speech was being enlarged, where their lapses into offensive religious speech could be treated as exceptions that proved a greater rule. *Cantwell* had done the heavier work of limiting the authority of the state to regulate the propagation of religious speech; *Chaplinsky* merely identified occasions when offensive speech directed at individual targets could be penalized. A decision allowing the Witnesses to go their zealous way would not revive the pervasive incivility that had plagued Reformation Europe. It merely illustrated how a liberal, tolerant society could indulge offensive outbursts of religious enthusiasm.

In pursuing this course, however, the Supreme Court did not privilege the Free Exercise clause per se. Rather, it treated claims of conscience and exercise as elements of or supplements to broader conceptions of freedom of speech and press. The burden of proof lay less on religious advocates having to demonstrate their right to express their views than on officials seeking to protect their authority to regulate or moderate public speech, whatever its content. As Ira Lupu and Robert Tuttle have succinctly observed:

> The Court did not view the [Witnesses'] cases as involving specifically religious messages or speakers. Instead, the Court framed the issues in more general terms, and focused on constitutional control over the discretionary power of local officials to favor or disfavor particular causes. Accordingly, the Court used these cases to establish a set of enduring principles about the rights of political, social, or religious proselytizers to be free of such censorial discretion.[38]

One can speculate why the Justices found this reliance on general conceptions of the freedom of speech so attractive. That reliance would liberate courts from having to assess the demands of ardent sectarians or to defend religious views that offended the larger community. Nor would courts need to ask how important a particular religious claim was, to determine "whether the religious practice at issue is central or peripheral, obligatory or customary, subject to rewards or pains in the hereafter," or whether it was being expressed with true sincerity.[39] If one adopts the perspective of Jefferson and Madison, the logic of these decisions would preserve the desired privacy of religious belief and behavior, minimizing the need for the state to deal with religion at all.

There is perhaps an even deeper irony in this juxtaposition. If one assumes that freedom of religious expression preceded and thus encouraged the opening up of political and cultural speech, by the mid-twentieth century religious speech was being relegated to a lower level of importance. It was becoming just one example of the multiple forms of expression a liberal polity should protect. Adherents of ardent religious beliefs might prefer to have their convictions earn formal legal recognition, but from the vantage point of jurisprudence, secular justifications offer a safer, more prudent rationale.

### EXEMPTIONS AND ACCOMMODATIONS

Taking this long view, the novelty of the Witnesses' cases hinges not on the kind of religious activity they represented, but rather on their role in advancing such judicial concepts as the incorporation of the Bill of Rights under the Fourteenth Amendment or the need to protect "discrete and insular minorities" lacking recourse to the political system. The true development of the modern conception of the free exercise of religion followed a different trajectory. This one was concerned not with the candid expression of controversial religious beliefs, but with the invocations of norms of religious freedom to insulate or exempt individuals from compliance with ordinary law.

Two decades passed between the heyday of the Witnesses' litigation in the late 1930s and early 1940s and the appearance of exemption doctrine, which seeks to provide some accommodation between the public interest of the state and the claims of religiously scrupulous individuals. The key terms at work here are *exemption* and *accommodation*, which respectively represent the conscience claims of individuals and the flexibility of the state. The subject remains hotly contested today, the source of an ever-increasing array of judicial decisions and a vast archive of scholarly articles. No historian can pretend to do justice to this subject, but a short narrative can provide a basis for critical reflection.

That narrative would begin with the lead case of *Sherbert v. Verner* (1963), which was foreshadowed by the 1961 case, *Braunfeld v. Brown*.[40] In *Braunfeld* an Orthodox Jewish furniture storeowner challenged a recent Pennsylvania statute creating a Sunday closing law, on the grounds that a mandatory closing on the Christian Sabbath imposed serious costs that placed his entire business at risk because of his religion. A divided Court narrowly upheld the statute. In his plurality opinion Chief Justice Earl Warren invoked the conventional distinction between beliefs and actions posited in *Reynolds v. U.S.* while also citing Jefferson's 1802 letter to the Danbury Baptists, which contrasted one's natural right to opinions from "social duties" subject to regulation. Jewish merchants might well suffer an economic burden, Warren conceded, but their ability to practice their religion would not be affected. A "general law" enacted to pursue "secular goals" would remain "valid despite its indirect burden on religious observance unless the State may accomplish its purpose by means which do not impose such a burden."

The secular goal was obviously not a Christian desire to sanctify the Sabbath but rather a laudable policy of making one day of the week an occasion for "rest, repose, recreation, and tranquility," a collective day of leisure that hardly resembled a seventeenth-century Puritan Sunday.[41] In a partial dissent, Justice William Brennan disputed the "rational basis" standard on which the Court accepted the legislature's decision to make Sunday the state's day of "tranquility." The burden imposed on the Jewish storekeepers was significant, while the imagined harm to the state affected only "the mere convenience of having everyone rest on the same day," producing putative benefits that Brennan thought "more fanciful than real."[42]

Two years later, Brennan wrote the majority opinion in *Sherbert*. The plaintiff was a Seventh Day Adventist who lost her job in a South Carolina textile mill after her employer turned a five-day work week into six days of labor. Because Adventists also made Saturday their Sabbath, Adeil Sherbert (like Braunfield) would not violate the fourth commandment. After her search for other work failed for this same reason, her application for twenty-two weeks of unemployment compensation was also denied, first by the state commission, then by the state supreme court. She then appealed the case to the Supreme Court, asserting that these denials violated her free exercise of religion.

Justice Brennan's opinion appears reasonably straightforward. First, and arguably most important, he endorsed Sherbert's claim. Forcing her to avoid adhering to "the precepts of her religion in order to accept work" would "impose the same kind of burden upon the free exercise of religion as would a fine imposed against the appellant for her Saturday worship." Because the state already exempted workers from being compelled to labor on Sunday, the denial of benefits to a Sabbatarian was discriminatory.[43] Second, South Carolina could adduce no "compelling state interest" to justify "the substantial infringement" of Sherbert's rights. In *Braunfield* the state of Pennsylvania could not have attained its policy end without designating one day as the day of leisure. By contrast, in *Sherbert* the best objection the state offered was to worry about "fraudulent claims by unscrupulous claimants feigning religious objections to Saturday work." The state could deal with that problem without impairing Sherbert's rights of conscience. Third, a decision favoring the Sabbatarians would do nothing to establish Seventh Day Adventists as a religion. It would merely treat their concerns with the same "neutrality" owed to all faiths and denominations.

*Sherbert* is not a lengthy decision, but it was long enough to establish a three-pronged test for assessing apparent government assaults on the free exercise of religion: Was there a genuine burden on religious behavior? Did the state have a compelling interest in executing its policy? Were less obstructive means available to attain its ends?

Had these three tests been applied to Billy and Lilian Gobitas in 1935, their practicality would have been evident. The burden on their consciences was transparent; *pace* Justice Frankfurter, one could easily argue that the state lacked a compelling interest in universal flag salutes; and even if a patriotic case could be made, the children's willingness to stand silently during the salute showed that a less obstructive option was available.

Unlike the Flag Salute cases, which were a latter-day version of the flashpoint confrontations that vexed Reformation Europe, *Braunfield* and *Sherbert* covered realms of behavior where the modern state was a more active force. Had no system of unemployment compensation existed, Sherbert could simply have been fired without any legal recourse. But unemployment compensation, even for a limited period, was an element of the modern welfare state, and if religion offered some discriminatory basis for distributing its benefits, why should the state commission's decisions not be subject to constitutional challenge?

More importantly, *Sherbert* marks the starting point for a modern jurisprudence of accommodations and exemptions. As Lupu and Tuttle observe, its reliance on the Free Exercise clause alone to authorize noncompliance with generally applicable laws did mark a radical departure in jurisprudence. "It is vital to see that this prin ciple had never before appeared in our constitutional law," they remark. Prior cases, including *Cantwell*, *Barnette*, and *Reynolds*, had relied on "general theories of constitutional rights" that did not elevate religious motives above other concerns. But the logic of *Sherbert* had the effect of "privileging religiously motivated conduct over its secular analogues" while raising difficult questions about "the state's competence" to assess how burdensome these conditions actually were. Sabbatarian concerns were easy to assess, but other issues might prove far more difficult.[44] On the other hand, for anyone concerned with protecting the rights of religious minorities holding views that mainstream observers find extreme or absurd—and Adventists descend from the Millerite movement that awaited the Second Coming on October 22, 1844, but instead experienced the "Great Disappointment"—the egalitarian commitment of *Sherbert* offers an admirable balancing test.[45]

In fact, *Sherbert* did not lead to a preferential approach for religious exemptions. Its consequences were largely limited to the realm of unemployment compensation, an innocuous form of social welfare that operates only for brief periods. A far stronger basis for asserting a broad right of religious exemption came with *Wisconsin v. Yoder*. Here the state sued a group of Old Order Amish parents who wanted their children to be released from obligatory school attendance at age fourteen, rather than the sixteen that Wisconsin required. The parents cited the Free Exercise Clause in their defense. Attending secondary school would not only interfere with the communal and vocational duties Amish children should learn. It would also "endanger their salvation and that of their parents" and pose "a very real threat of undermining the Amish community and religious practice as they exist today," a threat so severe that the Amish "must either abandon belief and be assimilated into society at large or be forced to migrate to some other and more tolerant region."[46]

The opinions in *Wisconsin v. Yoder*—with Chief Justice Warren Burger writing for a six-justice majority, two concurring opinions written by Justices Potter Stewart and Bryon White, and Justice William Douglas partially dissenting—are conceptually more robust than the comparable statements in *Braunfeld* and *Sherbert*. To some extent, they are also more salient to our concerns. The opinions directly invoke the Free Exercise Clause to address the collective rights of the Amish as a sectarian community with a long history, and within a context that recognizes both the growing regulatory authority of the modern state and the autonomy of the school-age youths who were not yet full members of their families' church. Descending from the Anabaptist Mennonites of the early sixteenth century, the Amish rivaled the Quakers in carrying some of the most radical convictions of the Reformation into American culture. Yet the situation of their children echoed concerns that Locke and Jefferson had considered. And to the Amish way of thinking, their families would be placed in a situation akin to the one the Huguenots had faced during the 1680s.

The majority opinion in *Yoder* relied on "the unchallenged testimony of acknowledged experts in education and religious history"; a respectful, even romantic portrayal of Amish community life; and a skeptical assessment of the state's claim for additional education.[47] The majority held that no "compelling" public interest warranted adding two more years to the children's schooling. The vocational education they would receive at home would suit the real lives they would lead. Should the children choose to leave the faith, their "qualities of reliability, self-reliance, and dedication to work" would stand them well "in today's society." Any inferences to the contrary were "speculative" only. True, education had long been regarded as a fundament of republican citizenship, going back at least to the writings of Thomas Jefferson. Yet as Chief Justice Burger also noted, "When Thomas Jefferson emphasized the need for education as a bulwark of a free people against tyranny, there is nothing to indicate he had in mind compulsory education through any fixed age beyond a basic education."[48]

The majority was less confident in dealing with the challenge raised directly in Justice Douglas's dissent and echoed in the two concurrences. The majority opinion treated the three children involved in the case as ciphers. The dispute involved their parents and the state. The question of whether the children had an independent interest in pursuing their education went largely unexamined. Only one of the children had affirmed her desire to leave school; the views of the other two were not known (though they would have been unlikely participants in the litigation had their views differed from those of their parents). On this basis, the majority saw no reason to triangulate the question, to admit that there were three potential parties to the case, not two.

Justice Douglas, in dissent, thought the case should be remanded to learn the children's preferences. The Court could not unthinkingly "impose the parents' notion of religious duty on their children," who had reached an age where they were "'persons' within the meaning of the Bill of Rights."[49] The case was analogous to *Tinker v. Des Moines School District*,[50] a recent decision in which the Court had affirmed the free political speech of other young adolescents. Nor should the Court naively assume that their occupational futures would be secure should they abandon their faith. Foregoing a modern education at age fourteen would cripple a child's ability to pursue numerous opportunities, so that "his entire life may be stunted and deformed."[51] In their concurring opinions, Justices Stewart and White expressed some latent sympathy with Douglas's concerns, but concluded that the absence of significant testimony from the students and the depiction of the community's interests were enough to resolve the case.

The historian is tempted to follow the legal scholar Marci Hamilton in thinking that what saved the day for the parents and their community was an "admiration or nostalgia for certain religious beliefs, including their biblical basis, as much as any neutral legal principles."[52] The Amish were not obnoxious in the way that seventeenth-century Quakers and twentieth-century Jehovah's Witnesses had been, nor were they aggressive like the Mormon owners of a new Dispensation that superseded all others. They were attractive remnants of another age, bearers of a "primitivist" religiosity that had once flourished in America's radical Protestant sects.[53] To grant them a modest variation from Wisconsin's education requirements was less an act of toleration, in the traditional sense of accepting a hateful burden, than of laudable charity. Had the trial record been different—had the Court viewed the children as victims of their parents' ardor—the case might have turned another way. But the concurring justices, having stated a lingering qualm or two, were content with the outcome.

And yet: If one follows the admirable logic of the Douglas dissent, the problem of defining the "compelling" interest of the state attains real vitality. Why is it not equally a matter of public concern to maximize the opportunities available to every youth, and not to consign some to a narrow range of vocations to satisfy the religious preferences of their families and communities? In Marci Hamilton's take-no-prisoners view, *Yoder* "trivialized the impact on children of being forced by their parents' faith to leave school before the vast majority of other children."[54] When Burger suggested that the Amish embodied the virtues of the "'sturdy yeomen'" whom Jefferson idealized, he neglected to mention that Jefferson also divided the mass of the population "into two classes, the laboring & the learned."

Three years of primary schooling would take care of the former; it was the education of the latter, at the proposed University of Virginia, that dominated his concern.[55] His famous image of the yeoman farmer conveyed the same "'idyllic agrarianism'" that irritated Justice Douglas.[56] It bore no serious resemblance to the structure of a modern economy, nor could it capture the resources that liberty-wielding individuals would have to possess to pursue an occupation of their own choosing.

Equally important, as a pioneering acolyte of public education, Jefferson did possess a coherent conception of the stages of a child's enlightenment. He would not have taught children the alphabet with the stick-figure illustrations that accompanied the earliest versions of the celebrated, massively best-selling *The New-England Primer*:

A In *Adams'* fall, we sinned all
B Thy life to mend, This Book [the Bible] attend

If religious instruction were to be introduced at all in public schools, it should be done only later, after students (boys and girls alike) had read enough history to have a critical framework for assessing claims of religious truth. Here, again, Jefferson tracked Locke's position in the *Letter Concerning Toleration* that the point of education—and indeed of parentage—was to enable children to reach an age when they would be capable of ascertaining their own norms of religious truth or faith. Parents did not have a property right governing their children's religious commitments. They were not the owners of their children's religious beliefs but rather the trustees of their intellectual development. True, it was the parents, not the magistrate, who had the opportunity and responsibility for conveying religious beliefs to the next generation. But the choice of faith could never be theirs. "Nothing can be imagined more absurd," Locke argued, than to assume that "the Religion of Parents would descend unto Children, by the same right of Inheritance as their Temporal Estates."

## THE ROAD TO RFRA

The development of free exercise doctrine in the immediate post-*Yoder* years did not take a dramatic course. The exceptional nature of the Amish community limited *Yoder*'s impact. Had the Court been more enthusiastic in the cause of enlarging religious freedom, and more sensitive to the distinctive needs of marginal religious groups, it could have endorsed the comparable claims of three Native American communities to protect lands they regarded as sacred space from timbering and road-building activities the National Forest Service had approved. Yet in *Lyng v. Northwest Indian Cemetery* (1988),[57] the Court upheld the Forest Service's decision, even though it was difficult to identify any "compelling" public interest in using the specific tracts in dispute.[58] A few other decisions also merit mentioning. In *Bob Jones University v. U.S.* (1983),[59] the Court held that the Free Exercise Clause did not justify granting tax exempt status to a fundamentalist institution that engaged in racially discriminatory practices by prohibiting interracial dating and marriage. Three years later, in *Goldman v. Weinberger*,[60] a narrowly divided Court held that the Air Force had not violated the clause by prohibiting Simcha Goldman, an ordained rabbi and clinical psychologist, from wearing his yarmulke while on duty. A year later, Congress enacted legislation to permit such an exception.

Yet independently of this apparent judicial quiescence, developments were afoot that would help to transform free exercise jurisprudence. Cases involving both parts of the Religion Clause continued to flow to the Court, in turn generating a flow of academic efforts to assess, critique, dissect, endorse, and oppose the ensuing opinions and dissents. The complexity of the tests the Court was applying inspired, provoked, and sometimes inflamed the ideological and intellectual commitments that carry legal scholars into academic battle. Moreover, although it is difficult to measure the impact that scholarship actually exerts on judicial decisions, enterprising academics often hope that an influential article can entice courts into considering new arguments.

One scholar who manifestly achieved this end was Michael McConnell. In 1985, when he was a starting assistant professor at his professional alma mater, the University of Chicago Law School, McConnell published a seminal essay on the "Accommodation of Religion." His controlling thesis was "that between the accommodations compelled by the Free Exercise Clause and the benefits to religion prohibited by the Establishment Clause there exists a class of permissible government actions toward religion, which have as their purpose and effect the facilitation of religious liberty." This emphasis on the promotion of religious liberty, rather than the maintenance of a high wall of separation between church and state, represented the best "interpretation grounded in the political theory of the Constitution."[61] Five years later, McConnell published a second lengthy essay on "The Origins and Historical Understanding of Free Exercise of Religion." Here he argued that the original understanding supported the idea that religious convictions provided a legitimate basis for seeking exemptions from secular law. This story gave special emphasis to Madison, and particularly to key passages in his *Memorial and Remonstrance*. By contrast, the views of Locke and Jefferson were far less supportive of this position.[62]

Although much of McConnell's argument was clearly doctrinal in nature, historical and normative claims were also fundamental to his case.[63] "It is sometimes forgotten that religious liberty is the central value and animating purpose of the Religion Clauses of the First Amendment," he began. Religious liberty consisted primarily

of "the autonomy of religious institutions, individual choice in matters of religion, and the freedom to put a chosen faith (if any) into
practice." By contrast, the "separation of church and state" was "a
more problematical, a more contingent, ideal," something that could
either "enhance" or "diminish" religious liberty. Where many commentators might casually equate disestablishment and separation,
McConnell's idea of accommodation clearly distinguished them.[64]
McConnell also offered a "pluralist" account of American religion
that he deemed "more consistent than its competitors with the liberal political theory which underlies the Constitution." That theory
had to recognize inter alia that some citizens might feel bound to
obey "higher claims than those of government" and that "the liberal
state has no direct means of shaping the nation's moral thinking."
In such a regime, the positive contribution of religion to civic virtue
could lower Jefferson's wall of separation and deny the contention
that government must always adopt a position of "strict neutrality"
that gave religion no distinctive status.[65]

There is much to dispute in McConnell's account. Consider his
claim that "while unable to establish a national religion, the liberal
state cannot also reject in principle the possibility that a religion may
be true; and if true, religious claims are of a higher order than anything in statecraft."[66] One can as easily argue that the impossibility
of verifying or falsifying religious truth is what requires the liberal
state to recognize only the interior, subjective claims of belief and
conscience that are the essence of Protestant religiosity. Similarly,
the idea that Madison wanted "to foster strong and vigorous religion" as a source of republican virtue does not wholly conform to
the arch comments one finds in his important 1787 memorandum on
the Vices of the Political System of the United States. Here Madison
gave religion a double billing as both "a motive to oppression as
well as a restraint on injustice." Refining the point six months later,
Madison concluded that "Even in its coolest state, [religion] has

been much more oftener a motive to oppression than a restraint from it."[67] This was not only the old fear of "priestcraft" that Madison shared with Jefferson and Locke. It also marked his emerging concern with the dynamics of public opinion—that is, with the attitudes of citizens at large.

Putting these historian's quibbles aside, one must still concede that McConnell's essays on accommodation had a powerful impact on this realm of legal thinking. That remained true three decades after he launched this project, even when arguments for moderate and constructive forms of accommodation were giving way to more strident and contentious calls for exemption.[68] The critical turning point occurred just as McConnell's essay on the original understanding of free exercise was going to press, and it pushed legal doctrine in a direction exactly opposite from the one he was exploring.[69]

The occasion was the Supreme Court's holding in *Employment Division v. Smith*,[70] arguably the most important modern ruling in free exercise jurisprudence. In this case, a drug rehabilitation clinic in Portland, Oregon, had fired two of its counselors after they confessed to ingesting peyote, a bitter-tasting cactus with powerful physiological and psychological effects. Peyote was the central sacrament in the rites of the Native American Church. When the Oregon Employment Division rejected their claim for unemployment compensation, they filed a civil suit, and the state supreme court ultimately upheld their claim, invoking the Free Exercise Clause as a legitimating factor in their request for compensation. But the state attorney general, David Frohnmayer, favored the strict enforcement of Oregon drug laws. While other states had accepted the use of peyote for religious purposes, Oregon still treated it as a prohibited hallucinogen. Frohnmayer appealed the decision to the US Supreme Court, and to almost everyone's surprise, its decision in what should have been a prosaic case, proved transformative.[71]

*Employment Division v. Smith* is remarkable for several reasons. It offers a curious illustration of the complexity of American federalism to witness a state attorney general, acting on his own convictions, appeal a judgment of his state's highest court to the US Supreme Court. It is even more striking to see a landmark constitutional ruling being rendered without the parties to the case or an array of interested observers having any sense that the suit carried this vast inflationary potential. The outcome stupefied the two lawyers who argued the decisive round of the case. "Was I there?" Smith's lawyer, Craig Dorsay, wondered after he learned of the decision. Dorsay and Frohnmayer had assumed the case would be decided in conformity with the "compelling interest" standard of *Sherbert*.[72] Instead, Justice Scalia's majority opinion abandoned the three decades of jurisprudence that had followed *Sherbert* and effectively restored *Reynolds v. U.S.*, the Mormon polygamy case, as the basic interpretation of the free exercise of religion.

In the first round of argument, the justices struggled over the importance to the Oregon supreme court of the legality of the use of peyote. The Oregon court had relied on the free exercise claim to argue that Smith was entitled to unemployment compensation, while noting that he had not been prosecuted for his ostensibly illegal activity. Yet the question remained: could the Court use a free exercise claim to overcome a criminal statute?[73] The Supreme Court remanded the case to resolve this question. In response, the state court conceded that Oregon law "makes no exception for the sacramental use of peyote," but it still adhered to its original rationale, again holding that the Free Exercise Clause permitted the ritual use of the drug and that Smith was entitled to unemployment compensation.

Frohnmayer again appealed to the Supreme Court. When the case was reargued on November 6, 1989 (coincidentally Al Smith's seventieth birthday), Frohnmayer argued that the state had a compelling need to have a uniform policy on controlled substances, while also warning that to grant a special dispensation to Native American peyote users would give their religious beliefs a public preference. Dorsay emphasized that the state had failed to intro- duce any evidence of the harmful effects of the ceremonial use of peyote, thereby implying that it had not identified the compelling interest the exemption would infringe. The sharp questioning he received from Sandra Day O'Connor and Scalia indicated the dif- ficulties he faced.

Writing for a five-justice majority, Scalia laid down a relatively simple principle for determining when religious exemptions are constitutionally required, one that obviated any need for balancing tests or theories of accommodation. When a state enacts "a neutral, generally applicable regulatory law" that carries no animus against any religion, a claim for exemption must fail. "The free exercise of religion means, first and foremost, the right to believe and pro- fess whatever religious doctrine one desires," Scalia wrote. When free exercise also "involves not only belief and profession but the performance of (or abstention from) physical acts," any attempt by government to disapprove those acts for religious reasons would be unconstitutional. If idolatrous Jews were again "bowing down before a golden calf," the state had no basis for action. But here the respondents "seek to carry the meaning" of the free exercise clause "one large step further" by arguing for an exemption from a "concededly constitutional" law. The record of the Court's jurispru- dence, he maintained, going back to *Reynolds*, disproved that claim. Such an argument had prevailed only in "hybrid situation[s]" when a specifically religious argument could be linked to other constitu- tional protections.

In the second part of his opinion, Scalia effectively gutted the *Sherbert* doctrine. The only scenario in which it worked lay in the realm of unemployment compensation. In other areas where it had been applied, decisions of government had been sustained, not overturned. To extend *Sherbert* to cover a violation of criminal law would be absurd. Even worse, a general application of *Sherbert* would create a condition of near legal "anarchy" in which courts would have to evaluate the sincerity and importance of the religious claims of an increasingly diverse society. "What principle of law or logic can be brought to bear," Scalia almost sputtered, "to contradict a believer's assertion that a particular 'act' is central to his personal faith?"[74]

Although Scalia had the full support of a five justice majority, he did not speak for a united court. In her extended concurring opinion, Justice O'Connor accepted only the result while sharply rejecting Scalia's attack on *Sherbert*. The three other justices (Harry Blackmun, Brennan, and Thurgood Marshall) joined the free exercise elements of O'Connor's concurrence while filing a separate dissent written by Blackmun. In their view, the *Sherbert* framework remained a viable method for testing the strength of both the state's interest and the validity of the exemption. Ample evidence from the states that permitted the sacramental use of peyote proved that no "parade of horribles" would follow recognition of this single claim. Nor should the premier authority of the free exercise of religion depend on its "hybrid" association with other rights. Where Scalia had closed his opinion by suggesting that minority religious groups could still appeal to the democratic political process—thereby implicitly rejecting the logic of *Carolene Products*, footnote 4—Blackmun responded with the properly Madisonian position that "the First Amendment was enacted precisely to protect the rights of those whose religious practices are not shared by the majority and may be viewed with hostility."[75]

Counting to five is the first strategic rule of Supreme Court litigation, and the five-member majority in *Smith II*, consisting of Scalia, Chief Justice William Rehnquist, White, John Paul Stevens, and Anthony Kennedy, had thus unraveled the doctrinal authority of the *Sherbert* test. But given the universal astonishment over the Court's wholly unanticipated decision; the presence of an articulate four-vote minority; and the formation of a network of interest groups soon united as the Coalition for the Free Exercise of Religion (CFER), it was also inevitable that the *Smith* decision would spark a reconsideration of free exercise jurisprudence. Discussion of how to respond to *Smith* began immediately among a handful of attorneys from the American Civil Liberties Union, the National Council of Churches, and the Joint Baptist Committee. Morton Halperin, the ACLU lawyer, soon invited Representative Stephen Solarz to join the discussion, with a specific strategy in mind: to use Congress's authority under Section 5 of the Fourteenth Amendment to enact a statute restoring *Sherbert* doctrine as the guiding rule of free exercise jurisprudence.[76] Like Sections 2 of the Thirteenth and Fifteenth Amendments, Section 5 gave Congress the "power to enforce, by appropriate legislation, the provisions of this Article." If the Free Exercise clause had been "incorporated" against the states under the authority of Section 1 of the Fourteenth Amendment, why could Congress not enforce its claims?

Thus was born the strategy that ultimately led to the Religious Freedom Restoration Act (RFRA) of 1993.[77] Whether Section 5 could be used to sustain this effort remained a fair question. Good arguments could be mobilized to support the proposition, and everyone knew that the sections authorizing legislative enforcement of the Reconstruction amendments were framed by Republican Congresses that detested the Supreme Court's abysmal holding in *Dred Scott v. Sandford*. There was an initial agreement that such a statute should be phrased in general terms; it should not, for example, be designed to make a specific case for the use of peyote. On the other side of the question, groups representing the interest of American Catholics—and most prominently, the United States Catholic Conference—were wary that the proposed bill could provide an additional source of authority for the legitimacy of abortion.

Opposition from pro-life groups who hoped that *Roe v. Wade* would be overturned was the single most important factor that prevented the enactment of RFRA through 1992. Halperin's leading role in chairing the newly formed Coalition for the Free Exercise of Religion nurtured the suspicions of some of its pro-life members. The ACLU, Halperin's own organization, was a prominent supporter of reproductive rights. Although it was not entirely clear how RFRA could be deployed to pro-choice ends—as opposed, say, to the desire of pro-life physicians and nurses not to be compelled to assist in abortions—the contentious politics of the abortion question made this a difficult issue to resolve. In response to this concern, Halperin resigned his chairmanship of the Coalition, but pro-life objections continued to fester.[78]

Two developments, however, eventually shifted the political equation. First, the Supreme Court's June 1992 decision in *Planned Parenthood v. Casey* confirmed that *Roe v. Wade* remained the law of the land, and that RFRA would therefore not be enlisted as a new source of support. Second, where President George H. W. Bush had waffled on RFRA, Bill Clinton entered the White House as its active supporter. Given these facts, the opposition of Catholics and other pro-life organizations to RFRA abated, and the law was finally enacted in November 1993. Only three senators opposed the final version of the bill. The House adopted RFRA on a voice vote *nemine contradicente*. Under its terms, any government institution undertaking an action that "'substantially burdens' a 'sincerely held' religious belief or practice" would require the institution to demonstrate that it was pursuing a compelling public interest using the "least restrictive means" available.[79]

The political branches of the federal government had thus taken a decisive stand to make the *Sherbert* doctrine the controlling legislative standard as a matter of federal law. Would the Supreme Court accept that view? Did Congress have the constitutional authority to enact such legislation insofar as it reached far beyond what the Court had held in *Smith* the First Amendment requires? While academic controversy over RFRA began quickly, it often takes time and a dose of legal ingenuity to develop a case that the Court will find ripe for review. At the outset, RFRA did *not* precipitate a sweeping change in the framework of religious freedom. Many of the federal cases that invoked its authority concerned the claims of incarcerated criminals. Here it proved easy to determine either that a serious burden had not been imposed or that a compelling interest tied to the efficient operation of prisons did exist. And when intrusive restrictions on an innocuous religious practice were found, the identification of a less burdensome alternative was not so difficult. Although a sense of alarm that religious freedom would come under assault had permeated the response to *Smith*, the case record did not confirm that this was the situation. To the extent that did happen, how much of a benefit would RFRA provide?[80]

It took several years for the right test case to make its way to the Court. *City of Boerne v. Flores*[81] involved a suit in which the city council of Boerne, Texas, had rejected an application from a local Catholic church seeking to expand its facilities to serve its parishioners. The church lay within Boerne's historic district, and city officials favored matters of historic preservation over the church's concerns. Archbishop Flores of San Antonio sued the city, invoking RFRA on the grounds that the city was imposing a serious burden on the expression of religion. The city's initial strategy was to argue that historic preservation constituted a compelling state interest, but it then decided to go even further and to challenge the constitutionality of RFRA. The city's lawyers argued that Section 5 of the Fourteenth Amendment did not give Congress the power to impose this view of religious liberty on state and local governments.

The federal district court ruled in favor of the church, but after the Fifth Circuit reversed its decision, the city sought review in the Supreme Court. Two leading academics served as counsel for the opposing sides: Marci Hamilton, a leading critic of religious exemptions, represented the city,[82] while Douglas Laycock, who ranks with McConnell as the leading advocate for accommodations, represented the church.

Questions of compelling public interest and burdens on free exercise were at best minor motifs in the oral argument. The controlling issues were whether "Congress has the power to decree the substance of the [First] Amendment's restrictions on the States," beyond what the Court had held in *Smith*; and whether RFRA itself was a "proper exercise" of a congressional enforcement power. Considerations of federalism and the separation of powers both came into play. If RFRA was constitutional, and if any act of state and local government was therefore subject to review when individuals claimed a burden on their free exercise of religion, there would be no practicable limit on RFRA's potential scope, and Congress could then use its remedial or preventive power under Section 5 of the Fourteenth Amendment to enforce rights to enlarge its substantive authority over the Court's determination of their definition. Bearing the hallowed grail of *Marbury v. Madison* into its judgment, the Court insisted that it alone had the constitutional authority to define the content of constitutional rights. To allow congressional majorities to do that would derogate the super-majoritarian rules that were essential to American constitutionalism.

Justice Anthony Kennedy wrote the opinion for the six-member majority, striking down RFRA as it applied to state and local governments. Kennedy conceded that it "is not easy to discern" the line between a substantive definition of a right and measures for its enforcement. But precisely because that was the case, "There must be a congruence and proportionality between the injury to be prevented or remedied and the means adopted to that end."[83] In the majority's view, RFRA vastly exceeded those limitations. It imposed no significant limits on the laws and regulations that were now subject to review. Had the legislative and judicial history of RFRA demonstrated that religious bigotry was at loose in the land, its stringent standards might have been justified. But save for the lone case of *Church of Lukumi Babalu Aye v. Hialeah*,[84] which involved a deliberately anti-Santerian ordinance against the ritual slaughter of chickens, it was not clear what danger there was to fight.

Three justices dissented from the decision: Sandra Day O'Connor, Steven Breyer, and David Souter. O'Connor wrote the lengthiest dissent. Relying on McConnell's work on the original meaning of free exercise, she argued that the "Nation's Founders" had made "a profound commitment to religious liberty" that still warranted the "heightened protection" the pre-*Smith* doctrine had recognized. Breyer seconded most of O'Connor's dissent, and all three justices agreed that the issues in *Smith* needed to be properly presented and reargued. Rebutting O'Connor, Scalia wrote a lengthy concurrence reviewing the historical evidence, concluding that it was more "supportive" than "destructive" of the argument he had crafted in *Smith*.

While *Boerne* rejected the application of RFRA to the states, the statute still applies to acts of the national government. Exercising its vested legislative authority, Congress is fully competent to make past and future laws subject to RFRA restrictions. Of course, any future Congress could modify those restrictions by amending or repealing RFRA, because one legislature can never bind its successors. Perhaps a "vasty deep" of religious exemptions was waiting to be summoned into action, as RFRA's advocates supposed. But to paraphrase Hotspur scoffing Owen Glendower, the open question remained: would the courts "come when you do call for them"?[85]

The record suggests that Hotspur's skepticism provides a better metaphor for the impact of RFRA than Glendower's boasts of the "fiery shapes" and "burning cressets" that welcomed his birth. On the one hand, it is true that the cycle of episodes that extends from the procedural anomalies of *Smith*, to the coalition of forces supporting RFRA, to the limitation imposed by *Boerne*, to the enactment of state-based RFRAs, and finally to cases like *Hobby Lobby* and *Masterpiece Cakeshop* constitute a great tale of American constitutional history. It is a matter of regret that a definitive history of the RFRA cycle remains unwritten. On the other hand, it remains difficult to measure the effect that RFRA statutes have actually had on American religious freedom.

Early attempts to measure this impact have not produced dramatic conclusions about its effects. In the phrasing of the law schools, the criteria laid down in *Sherbert* and RFRA are standards, not rules, and "the endless plasticity of those standards," Ira Lupu observes, "invites widely disparate lines of argument for advocates and equally disparate modes of resolution for judges." This "plasticity," however, has been complicated and concentrated by the intense connections between an RFRA regime and the culturally urgent questions of same-sex marriage and abortion. Those questions inevitably invoke two other fundamental standards of American law: the "third-party" effects that individual or corporate claims for religious exemption have on other persons, and the robust commitment to anti-discrimination norms that has governed constitutional practice since the 1960s.[86]

In the decade after *Boerne*, the Supreme Court's one notable interpretation of RFRA occurred in *Gonzalez v. O Centro Espirita Beneficente do Vegetal*,[87] a case quite similar to *Employment Division v. Smith* because it involved the ritual use of hoasca, a tea containing an addictive controlled substance. Writing for a unanimous Court, Chief Justice John Roberts held that because the government had not established its compelling interest in denying any and all exceptions to the Controlled Substances Act, the use of hoasca was permissible. Yet if *Gonzalez* invited an application of RFRA highly friendly to religion, subsequent decisions by lower courts have not fulfilled that promise. As Lupu notes, "the record shows occasional outlier victories" for free exercise claims outmatched by "a stark pattern of defeats." A similar tendency emerged with state RFRA statutes. Although state and federal judges have entertained numerous RFRA based lawsuits, they typically "proceed with great caution and persistent deference to the government, despite RFRA's bold, religion-protective language."[88]

The major apparent departure from this trend came with the *Hobby Lobby* decision of 2014 and its strange sequel, *Zubik v. Burwell* (2017). In both cases, the Court entertained RFRA-based claims seeking exemptions from particular provisions of the Affordable Care Act (colloquially known as Obamacare) respectively requiring a family-owned private corporation and a cluster of religiously affiliated nonprofit organizations to provide contraceptive coverage to female employees through their group insurance plans. In both cases, the Supreme Court indicated that compliance with the "contraception mandate" would "substantially burden" the plaintiffs' exercise of religion. The Green family who are sole owners of the Hobby Lobby chain of stores are evangelical Christians, and that simple fact mitigated any qualm over asking whether a for-profit corporation actually exercised religion. *Zubik* assembled a coalition of evangelical and Catholic institutions with self-evident religious commitments. One difficulty in both cases—but especially in *Zubik*—is whether effective "workarounds" are available that will simultaneously preserve the full access to health services to which female employees are legally entitled while simultaneously assuaging the burdens invoked by the institutions.

At this writing, the shifting composition of the Supreme Court and the positions apparently favored by the Trump administration make the resolution of this conflict difficult if not impossible to predict (and properly schooled historians should be reluctant to predict *anything*). The Court's recent pronouncements on RFRA indicate that its conservative majority was inclined to make the government's compelling interest more difficult to prove, and complainants' claims of infringed religious freedom easier to assert. On balance, one suspects that the current Court (as constituted with the recent appointments of Neil Gorsuch and Brett Kavanagh) will be more inclined to favor religious claims for exemptions or accommodations over the countervailing interests of those who may be harmed or offended. Yet to the patient historian, the resolution of such legal contests number (to borrow a phrase from Madison imagining the outcome of the Constitutional Convention) "among the other arcana of futurity and [are] nearly as inscrutable as any of them."[89]

Commentators on both sides are nervous about the future. "*Hobby Lobby* dramatically expanded the strength and reach of RFRA," Frederick Mark Gedicks observes, "by enabling religious exemptions on the basis of alternatives that are practicably unavailable to implement even compelling government interests, and by requiring genuinely strict judicial scrutiny of religiously burdensome government actions."[90] On the other side, Douglas Laycock worries that the escalatory strategies that religious and secular blocs are pursuing will devolve into a simple conflict between the zealous enemies of sin and the egalitarian opponents of bigotry. Religious liberty remains a fundamental right, Laycock instructs us, and the key test of its survival asks the advocates of secular liberal values, "to the maximum extent possible, [to] spare conscientious objectors from violating their deeply held religious commitments." But such a concession, Laycock laments, demands a "mutual tolerance and political will" that seem conspicuously absent.[91]

[ 176 ]

## MADISON'S RAZOR

A historian *d'un certain âge* has no ready answers to this dilemma, no obvious lessons to apply quickly or easily. Constitutional ideas and doctrines have their own logic to develop, but a range of plausible positions is always available that justices can apply as they wish. Historians inhabit a world of contingency, where any day—or any decision—brings its own surprises. It does not take a great leap of historical imagination to conceive *Employment Division v. Smith* or *City of Boerne v. Flores* being decided the opposite way. Nor can historians say which doctrinal developments are correct, which flawed; they are happier explaining why certain disputes are destined to continue than to pioneer a path to their resolution. Yet there may be certain inferences that historians can draw, certain cautions they might raise, to temper our understanding of the issues we face and the difficulties we encounter.

The starting position has to be to recall the central historical achievement of the American approach to religious freedom: to couple a belief in the sovereign autonomy of individual rights of conscience and the free expression of religion with a collective desire to sever the official relationship between church and state. The former belief was already ingrained in American culture by the end of the colonial era; the latter ambition reflected the already weakened condition of the legally established churches. This convergence of individual belief and collective aspiration created the hothouse conditions that led to the Second Great Awakening and the confirmation of "the great truth" that had long stirred James Madison: "that Religion flourishes in greater purity, without than with the aid of Government." It was not Madison's and Jefferson's achievement to make this condition possible, notwithstanding the significance that we rightfully attribute to the Virginia Declaration of Rights, the defeat of the general assessment bill, and the enactment of the Statute for Religious Freedom. But they did grasp the constitutional importance of these events, and their writings, though concise, remained an authoritative source to later interpreters—ordinary citizens, politicians and jurists, and academic commentators.

That authority, however, does not cover the proposition that sustains the debate that originated with McConnell's essay on accommodation and the complicated legacy of *Employment Division v. Smith*. The idea that free exercise claims would broadly justify exemptions from ordinary law was manifestly *not* a legacy of Revolutionary-era thinking about the realm of religious freedom. True, there are a handful of statements in the historical record that can be interpreted to support this position. By far the most important appears in the opening item of Madison's *Memorial and Remonstrance*, with its strong assertion that "the duty" every person owes to "the Creator . . . is precedent, both in order of time and in degree of obligation, to the claims of Civil Society."

If one applies such statements deductively, as a priori general propositions to be directed against any law subjectively deemed burdensome to one's religious belief, then a historical basis for RFRA is well established. The great problem with this presumption is that Madison and his contemporaries were operating within the parameters that Locke had laid down in the opening pages of his *Letter Concerning Toleration*. "I esteem it above all things necessary," Locke asserted,

> to distinguish exactly the Business of Civil Government from that of Religion, and to settle the just Bounds that lie between the one and the other. If this be not done, there can be no end put to the Controversies that will be always arising, between those that have, or at least pretend to have, on the one side, a

Concernment for the Interest of Mens Souls, and on the other
side, a Care of the Commonwealth.

This distinction was not soft and flabby; it was clearly defined and
concisely stated. "*The Commonwealth* seems to be a Society of Men
constituted only for the procuring, preserving, and advancing of
their own *Civil Interests*," Locke continued, and those interests "I
call Life, Liberty, Health, and Indolency of Body; and the Possession
of outward things, such as Money, Lands, Houses, Furniture, and
the like."[92] When Madison considered issues of disestablishment
and free exercise a near century later, Locke's distinction remained
fundamental to his concerns, even though he and Jefferson believed
that Americans could go further. Civil government was one concern, salvation was another; and nothing the magistrate could do or
even think would have any effect on an individual's religious duty.
Madison's concerns never evolved into a discussion of whether the
"homage" one owed the Creator provided a valid basis for challenging the secular acts of civil government. Inhabiting an intensely
Protestant society, eighteenth-century Americans did not experience
the intense legalism that one associates with Islamic or Orthodox
Jewish life. As McConnell himself concedes, "the occasions when
religious conscience came into conflict with generally applicable
secular legislation were few." These occasions were essentially limited to "three issues: oath requirements, military conscription, and
religious assessment."[93]

None of these issues verges anywhere near our modern disputes
over exemptions and accommodations. None of them foresees how
the modern regulatory state, an entity the Founding generation
would have struggled to conceive, has transformed the entire framework of governance. None of them imagines the vast dominions of
modern medicine or of the range of treatments available to legions of
ailments. Most important, none of them imagines how the principle

of individual equality—the great if unintended consequence of Jefferson's Declaration of Independence—could challenge forms of hierarchy, privilege, and discrimination that once seemed enduring elements in the natural order of things, to the point where physical disability, perceived sexual "deviance," and an institution as familiar and essential as marriage would be reconceived in profoundly different ways. To ask how the founding generation would assess the case for religious exemptions without also giving them the same evidence and moral concerns that we possess and sometimes dispute exposes the futility of the exercise.

Yet inferences and insights are there to be drawn, and if they do not offer binding legal dictates, they still provide lessons worth pondering. Four of these seem especially salient.

The first of these concerns the third-party effects that necessarily arise when a claim for a religious exemption from a public law adversely affects other groups or individuals. In the apt phrasing of Douglas Nejaime and Reva Siegel, such "complicity-based conscience claims" threaten to impose "material and dignitary harms" on individuals who are not part of the claimant's "faith community." The claim for an exemption asserts that the behavior in question is sinful in nature, and that government cannot therefore compel individual to commit an act that compromises their convictions (and within a Christian community, their prospects for salvation).[94] Whether government should be mindful of sin, which is a religious rather than a legal concept, poses one problem with his approach.[95] But the more serious objection is why ordinary individuals pursuing their own "civil interests" should suffer for someone else's theology.

To the historian, it is puzzling to learn that the matter of third-party harms has not gained full recognition. Commentators who believe that the third-party variable deserves greater emphasis write as if that point still needs to be conclusively established. Not that the Supreme Court has been unmindful of this issue: Justice Samuel

Alito addresses it in footnote 37 in *Hobby Lobby*, though in terms that have drawn significant criticism.[96] Yet given the emphasis that claims of religious conscience enjoyed in the evolution of ideas of religious freedom in colonial America, this need seems surprising. Assume as we must that decisions over abortion and contraception do have a moral dimension, tied to one's conception of when life or personhood or (for that matter) the implantation of the soul begins, and that answers to these questions often (if not always) have a religious dimension. That perforce makes them matters of conscience, whether moral or avowedly religious. But the founding ideal of the American conception of free exercise rests on the radical devolution of spiritual autonomy to each individual (male and female He created them both). The exercise of conscience does not exhaust the realm of free expression, but it is its original principle, and its possession must be unalienable. "Conscience is the most sacred of all property," Madison observed in 1792; "other property depending in part on positive law, the exercise of that, being a natural and unalienable right." How could anyone alienate that right to someone else, and especially to another private party? How could the employee-beneficiary of health insurance transfer this moral decision to her employer-benefactor? If the grounds for employer preferences are manifestly religious, as they were for the Green family in *Hobby Lobby*, their exercise of that power over their employees would nonetheless remain inherently paternalist and inegalitarian.

The second concern relates to the premise or theory that underlies the dominant conception of our "Madisonian constitution,"—the term we regularly invoke to describe the original theory of our constitutional order. Following the logic of Madison's most celebrated essays, *Federalist* 10 and 51, this theory postulates that the best security for republican liberty lies in the jostling existence of a "multiplicity of factions" in society at large. The paradigmatic example of that multiplicity lay where Madison originally located it: in the disputatious nature of American Protestantism and the argumentative sects it had created. In an expanding, developing society like the early American republic, a similar variety of economic interests, many in competition and conflict with each other, would nonetheless create conditions that would provide a "republican remedy for the diseases most incident to republican government."[97]

Madison understood that there was one dangerous exception to this general theory: the possibility that the concentrated geographical presence or absence of slavery as a dominant economic condition would create antagonistic regional political blocs, allowing the heresies of nullification or secession to become plausible strategies of constitutional resistance. A year after his death on June 28, 1836, slavery was one of the issues that worked to fracture the Presbyterian Church into northern and southern branches. It proved even more important in the regional ruptures of Methodists and Baptists in the mid-1840s, which were quasi-secessionist movements of their own.[98] These divisions did not alter the underlying American commitment to religious freedom, but they illustrated and confirmed an ominous defect in Madison's constitutional theory.

Do today's conflicts over abortion and same-sex marriage pose a comparable challenge—if not a path to secession, then at least to the kinds of civic divisions that trouble Laycock? Opposition to both practices and to the legal arguments supporting them can take various forms that need not depend on religious convictions. One needs no theology to criticize the constitutional idea of a fundamental right to privacy that Justice Douglas sketched in the contraception case of *Griswold v. Connecticut* (1965), derived from metaphorical "penumbras, formed by emanations" from various "guarantees" in the Bill of Rights, and its later expansion in *Roe v. Wade*. Yet it would be foolish to deny that religious convictions have always informed and indeed dominated the passion that informs the debate over abortion, contraception, and same-sex marriage. The danger in these debates lies in its potential to create a binary opposition between the religiously motivated (faithful Catholics, evangelical Protestants, Orthodox Jews), on the one hand, and (for want of a more specific term) secular liberals and egalitarians, on the other. One doubts that the tensions between these two blocs will replicate the political mood of the 1850s, or produce a revolutionary scenario akin to Margaret Atwood's great dystopian novel (and popular television series) *A Handmaid's Tale*, now extended in its concluding sequel, *The Testaments*. Yet at the close of the second decade of the twenty-first century, the role of the evangelicals in American politics—and more specifically, their remarkably persistent support for President Trump, as woeful a sinner and morally wretched an individual as has ever occupied the White House—has become one of the great puzzles that perplex us. Madison envisioned a world in which a collective commitment to religious liberty would secure us all, because sects, denominations, and faiths would disagree with each other. That may not be the situation we now face.

Third, Madison's approach to the protection of rights in a constitutional republic rested on a deeply egalitarian understanding that argued that the great danger was not to protect the people as a whole against the concentrated power of the state, but to protect minorities and individuals against the opinions, passions, and interests of popular majorities. Claims of rights of conscience and free expression remain inherently egalitarian because they presuppose that each individual has the same moral capacity and duty to articulate his or her own articles of faith. This formulation remains relevant to our situation in two important respects. First, claims for religious exemptions and accommodations come not from the mainstream denominations that face no challenges to their status, but from smaller and more enthusiastic groups who feel their beliefs and behaviors are being besieged and indeed mocked and derided by a more secular, less devout majority who are indifferent to the just claims of the faithful. These claims are egalitarian in nature because they insist that their religious commitments deserve the same equal respect accorded to the more secular, less devout majority. The irony of this position, from the classic Madisonian perspective, is that these religious claims are most likely to prevail in the smaller communities where "factious majorities" can rule—say, those west Texas towns where well-organized evangelicals deem it perfectly appropriate to "solemnize" football games with a public prayer.

On the other side of this ledger, however, arguments against exemptions are also deeply egalitarian. Those who are now legally united in same-sex marriages rightfully insist that they are fully entitled to the same equality of legal rights and benefits that all married couples enjoy. Moreover, under the prevailing anti-discriminatory animus that has guided American law since the Civil Rights Act of 1964, that equality should govern their access to ordinary marketplace activities, such as the purchase of wedding cakes or the services of wedding photographers. Similar arguments apply to the reproductive rights concerns of women seeking contraceptive services or abortions: to deny them access to relevant information or necessary services would destroy the equality accorded to all patients. Once again, *contra* McConnell's claim, one could easily argue that the egalitarian commitments of the liberal state have the same authority as the faith-based obedience of the devout.

There is, finally, one other way to formulate a Madisonian response to our current dilemma. In *un petit hommage* to William of Occam, I will call this approach *Madison's razor*. The point of Occam's famous philosophical razor, in rather oversimplified terms, was to prefer explanations that were simpler and more parsimonious over those which were more complex. In a similar vein, we can reduce a putative Madison's razor of religious freedom to two postulates. First, the more we treat religion as a matter of private belief and voluntary associations that we pursue with other like-minded individuals, the more we appreciate it as a true wellspring of constitutional privacy, the better off we will be. Second, the more we allow the spheres of church and state to overlap, the more we lower Jefferson's proverbial wall of separation, the greater danger we run of viewing religion as one more sordid, corrupt interest. Locke's attempt to clearly distinguish the civil interests the commonwealth should protect from the spiritual concerns of voluntary religious societies remains, an exact third of a millennium later, a happy formula for civic peace.

Of course, many citizens and officials will often act on their religious convictions, and religious impulses have been an essential element in American politics, from the reform movements of the antebellum period to the modern civil rights movement to our current struggles over abortion. But the value of this contribution rests on its voluntary, noncoercive nature. For Madison as for Jefferson— as for Locke and Newton—the history of Christianity's relation with the state from the fourth century on was a tale of corruption, distortion, and injustice. The more one did to promote religion as the free exercise of personal conscience, the better off one would be. Madison summarized the great lesson in item eleven of the *Memorial and Remonstrance*:

Torrents of blood have been spilt in the old world, by vain attempts of the secular arm, to extinguish Religious discord, by proscribing all difference in Religious opinion. Time has at length revealed the true remedy. Every relaxation of narrow and rigorous policy, wherever it has been tried, has been found to assuage the disease. The American Theatre has exhibited proofs that equal and compleat liberty, if it does not wholly eradicate it, sufficiently destroys its malignant influence on the health and prosperity of the State.

This was more a statement of disestablishment than a positive affirmation of free exercise, but when one wields Madison's razor, the tension that modern commentators find between the Establishment and Free Exercise clauses dissipates. Disestablishment promoted free exercise, and free exercise made establishment superfluous.

That was the true and radical significance of the lively American experiment in religious freedom. Its lesson is one we should not ignore at a historical moment when religious violence is still slaughtering innocents by the thousands.

# Notes

. . .

INTRODUCTION

1. James Madison to Edward Livingston, July 10, 1822, in Jack Rakove, ed., *James Madison: Writings* (New York: Library of America, 1999), 789.

2. Madison to William Bradford, January 24, 1774, ibid., 7.

3. Richard Tuck, *The Sleeping Sovereign: The Invention of Modern Democracy* (Cambridge, UK: Cambridge University Press, 2015).

4. Julian P. Boyd, ed., *The Papers of Thomas Jefferson* (Princeton, NJ: Princeton University Press, 1950–), I: 548.

5. For perhaps the best illustration of this claim, see Kent Greenawalt, *Religion and the Constitution*, 2 vols. (Princeton, NJ: Princeton University Press, 2006, 2008); and Ira C. Lupu and Robert W. Tuttle, *Secular Government, Religious People* (Grand Rapids, MI: William B. Eerdmans, 2014).

6. This would be my short list (arranged alphabetically): Thomas J. Curry, *Farewell to Christendom: The Future of Church and State in America* (New York: Oxford University Press, 2001); Marc O. DeGirolami, *The Tragedy of Religious Freedom* (Cambridge, MA: Harvard University Press, 2013); Christopher L. Eisgruber and Lawrence G. Sager, *Religious Freedom and the Constitution* (Cambridge, MA: Harvard University Press, 2007); Noah Feldman, *Divided by God: America's Church-State Problem—And What We Should Do about It* (New York: Farrar, Straus and Giroux, 2005); Philip Hamburger,

*Separation of Church and State* (Cambridge, MA: Harvard University Press, 2002); Marci A. Hamilton, *God vs. the Gavel: Religion and the Rule of Law* (New York: Cambridge University Press, 2005); Andrew Koppelman, *Defending American Religious Neutrality* (Cambridge, MA: Harvard University Press, 2013); Isaac Kramnick and R. Laurence Moore, *The Godless Constitution: The Case against Religious Correctness* (New York: W. W. Norton and Co., 1996); Brian Leiter, *Why Tolerate Religion?* (Princeton, NJ: Princeton University Press, 2013); John T. Noonan Jr., *The Lustre of Our Country: The American Experience of Religious Freedom* (Berkeley: University of California Press, 1998); Martha C. Nussbaum, *Liberty of Conscience: In Defense of America's Tradition of Religious Equality* (New York: Basic Books, 2008); Stephen D. Smith, *Foreordained Failure: The Quest for a Constitutional Principle of Religious Freedom* (New York: Oxford University Press, 1995); Nelson Tebbe, *Religious Freedom in an Egalitarian Age* (Cambridge, MA: Harvard University Press, 2017). Of course, there are countless law review articles on these subjects, including a flotilla of essays by such scholars as Marci Hamilton, Ira Lupu, Douglas Laycock, my Stanford colleague Michael McConnell, Douglas Laycock, Mark Tushnet, and the trio of Richard Schragger, Micah Schwartzman, and Nelson Tebbe.

7. Compare the argument of David Sehat, *The Myth of American Religious Freedom* (New York: Oxford University Press, 2011), which emphasizes the pervasive authority of the "moral establishment," with various works by Steven K. Green, including *The Second Disestablishment: Church and State in Nineteenth-Century America* (New York: Oxford University Press, 2010), and *The Bible, the School, and the Constitution: The Clash That Shaped Modern Church-State Doctrine* (New York: Oxford University Press, 2012).

8. 374 U.S. 398 (1963).

9. 406 U.S. 205 (1972).

10. 494 U.S. 872 (1990).

11. 576 U.S.—(2015).

12. This judgment deserves some qualification, however, because arguments about the public expression of religious belief still remain controversial.

13. As Kent Greenawalt has observed, "one could never have expected religious claimants seeking exemptions to have the rate of success of persons challenging racial classifications or laws infringing freedom of speech." Greenawalt, *Religion and the Constitution*, 1: 30.

14. Alexandra Walsham, *Charitable Hatred: Tolerance and Intolerance in England, 1500–1700* (Manchester, UK: Manchester University Press, 2006), 261.

15. 381 U.S. 479 (1965).

## CHAPTER ONE

1. For one of many efforts to clarify these terms, see Andrew R. Murphy, "Tolerance, Toleration, and the Liberal Tradition," *Polity* 29 (1997), 593–623.

2. Walsham, *Charitable Hatred*, 1–5 (quotation at 4).

3. Anthony Pagden, *The Fall of Natural Man: The American Indian and the Origins of Comparative Ethnology* (New York: Cambridge University Press, 1982).

4. Stuart B. Schwarz, *All Can Be Saved: Religious Tolerance and Salvation in the Atlantic Iberian World* (New Haven, CT: Yale University Press, 2008). For one noteworthy expression of this belief, see Carlo Ginzburg, *The Cheese and the Worms: The Cosmos of a Sixteenth-Century Miller*, trans. John and Anne C. Tedeschi (Baltimore: The Johns Hopkins University Press, 1980), 47–49.

5. Perez Zagorin, *Ways of Lying: Dissimulation, Persecution, and Conformity in Early Modern Europe* (Cambridge, MA: Harvard University Press, 1990).

6. John Kilcullen and Chandran Kukathas, eds., *Pierre Bayle: A Philosophical Commentary on These Words of the Gospel, Luke 14:23, "Compel Them to Come In, That My House May Be Full"* [1686] (Indianapolis: Liberty Fund, 2015).

7. Perez Zagorin, *How the Idea of Religious Toleration Came to the West* (Princeton, NJ: Princeton University Press, 2003), 93–144.

8. See Mark Goldie, ed., *John Locke: A Letter Concerning Toleration and Other Writings* (Indianapolis: Liberty Fund, 2010), xxix–xxxii on the preparation of the texts.

9. Compare the concise survey by Zagorin, *How the Idea of Religious Toleration Came to the West*, with the four volumes of W. K. Jordan, *The Development of Religious Toleration in England* (Cambridge, MA: Harvard University Press, 1932–1940), which was completed when Jordan was all of thirty-eight (!); or John Marshall, *John Locke, Toleration, and Early*

*Enlightenment Culture* (Cambridge, UK: Cambridge University Press, 2006), a work whose 719-page analysis was reportedly slimmed down from a much heftier manuscript. For another insightful survey, which gives pride of place to Locke and Voltaire while extending the analysis into our own time, see Denis Lacorne, *The Limits of Tolerance: Enlightenment Values and Religious Fanaticism*, trans. C. Jon Delogu and Robin Emlein (New York: Columbia University Press, 2019).

10. In using this notion of "work," I draw upon David Nirenberg, *Anti-Judaism: The Western Tradition* (New York: W. W. Norton and Co., 2013), which repeatedly asks, what "work" did arguments of Anti-Judaism (as opposed to Anti-Semitism) perform in disputes that had nothing to do with Judaism per se.

11. Benjamin Kaplan, *Divided by Faith: Religious Conflict and the Practice of Toleration in Early Modern Europe* (Cambridge, MA: Harvard University Press, 2007). One could half-waggishly suggest that "tolerance" should replace "toleration" in the subtitle.

12. Nicholas Terpstra, *Religious Refugees in the Modern World: An Alternative History of the Reformation* (New York: Cambridge University Press, 2015) is very helpful on this point; and see Bernard Dompnier, *Le Venin de l'Hérésie: Image du Protestantisms et Combat Catholique au XVII Siècle* (Paris: Le Centurion, 1985).

13. Kaplan, *Divided by Faith*, 48–98.

14. Ibid., 73–79.

15. Ibid., 144–234.

16. Ibid., 15–47.

17. Brad S. Gregory, *Salvation at Stake: Christian Martyrdom in Early Modern Europe* (Cambridge, MA: Harvard University Press, 1999).

18. See the cautious discussion of this issue in Kaplan, *Divided by Faith*, 276–293.

19. Philip Benedict, *"Un Roi, Une Loi, Deux Fois*: Parameters for the History of Catholic-Reformed Co-existence in France, 1555–1685," in *Tolerance and Intolerance in the European Reformation*, ed. Ole Peter Grell and Bob Scribner (Cambridge, UK: Cambridge University Press, 1996), 65–93.

20. For one nuanced account of the complicated ways in which an individual family responded to this persecution, see Carolyn Chappell Lougee, *Facing the Revocation: Huguenot Families, Faith, and the King's Will* (New York: Oxford University Press, 2017).

21. *The Humble Address of the Distressed Protestants in France, As It Was Delivered to the French King* (London, 1681), 3. The *Address* was published in both English and French.

22. For a brief refresher in monarchical history: The childless Elizabeth was the last Tudor monarch. Upon her death in 1603, the throne passed to James VI of Scotland, the son of Mary Queen of Scots, who now also became James I of England. His son Charles I came to the throne in 1625, fought a civil war against his parliamentary and Puritan opponents, and was executed in 1649. Cromwell, a lead general of the revolutionary New Model Army, ultimately disbanded Parliament and ruled as the Lord Protector until his death in 1658. Charles II, the son of the executed king, was restored to the throne in 1660. His younger (and Catholic) brother, James, Duke of York, acceded to the throne in 1685, and was deposed by the Glorious Revolution, which brought the Protestant Dutch stadtholder, William of Orange, and his wife Mary, the Protestant daughter of James II, to the throne.

23. Ethan H. Shagan, *The Rule of Moderation: Violence, Religion and the Politics of Restraint in Early Modern England* (Cambridge, UK: Cambridge University Press, 2011), 15, 17.

24. Blair Worden, "Toleration and the Protectorate," in *God's Instruments: Political Conduct in the England of Oliver Cromwell* (New York: Oxford University Press, 2012), 64–67.

25. Walsham, *Charitable Hatred*, 84–86, 261.

26. See Andrew R. Murphy, *Liberty, Conscience, and Toleration: The Political Thought of William Penn* (New York: Oxford University Press, 2016), 56–83 for an interpretive rendering of the significance of this trial. *Bushel's Case*, holding that a juror could not be punished for his verdict, was a sequel to the Penn-Mead trial.

27. Murphy has a good short summary of the penal and Test Acts; see ibid., 161.

28. Steven Pincus, *1688: The First Modern Revolution* (New Haven, CT: Yale University Press, 2009), 142.

29. The most important recent work is Pincus, *1688*, which provides a bold, comprehensive, and pronouncedly revisionist history of the entire subject, broadly defined.

30. Scott Sowerby, *Making Toleration: The Repealers and the Glorious Revolution* (Cambridge, MA: Harvard University Press, 2013), 25.

31. This relationship is extensively covered in Murphy, *Liberty, Conscience, and Toleration*, 158–202. Penn was accused of being a secret Catholic; ibid., 190.

32. Sowerby, *Making Toleration*, 40–44; Murphy, *Liberty, Conscience, and Toleration*, 194–197.

33. Pincus, *1688*, 198–209.

34. Ibid., 143.

35. Ibid., 179–198, 228.

36. Shagan, *Rule of Moderation*, 288, and Walsham, *Charitable Hatred*, 267, both apply the modifier "misleadingly" to the imputed title of the act

37. Newton's intense religious life, including his apocalyptic obsessions, is brilliantly examined in Robert Iliffe, *Priest of Nature: The Religious Worlds of Isaac Newton* (New York: Oxford University Press, 2017).

38. For various recent accounts, see Sowerby, *Making Toleration*, 249–255; Walsham, *Charitable Hatred*, 267–269; Pincus, *1688*, 425–434.

39. John Marshall, *John Locke: Resistance, Religion, Responsibility* (New York: Cambridge University Press, 1994), 357–383. In this and the following paragraphs, I largely rely on Marshall's very careful exploration of Locke's life and views.

40. Ibid., 3–6.

41. For an overview of Locke's thoughts on theology near the close of his life, see ibid., 384–451.

42. Ibid., 12–21 (quotation defining "indifferent things" at 15).

43. Ibid., 62–72.

44. J. C. Walmsley and Felix Waldmann, "John Locke and the Toleration of Catholics: A New Manuscript," *The Historical Journal*, 62 (2019), 1093–1115.

45. On the impact of the sojourn in Holland on Locke's thinking, see Marshall, *Locke, Toleration, and Early Enlightenment Culture*, 469–535. For further discussion of Locke, see Teresa Bejan, *Mere Civility: Disagreement and the Limits of Toleratrion* (Cambridge, MA: Harvard University Press, 2017), 112–143; and Lacorne, *Limits of Tolerance*, 11–30.

46. David Como, *Radical Parliamentarians and the English Civil War* (Oxford: Oxford University Press, 2018), 302–305.

47. Goldie, ed., *Letter Concerning Toleration*, 12–15.

48. See, for example, the brief essay by the leading scholarly advocate of Spinoza's impact on the Radical Enlightenment: Jonathan Israel, "Spinoza,

Locke and the Enlightenment Battle for Toleration," in *Enlightenment in Toleration Europe*, ed. Ole Peter Grell and Roy Porter (Cambridge, UK: Cambridge University Press , 2000), 102–113. Chapter 7 of Zagorin, *How the Idea of Religious Toleration Came to the West*, 240–288, offers a very helpful Bayle–Locke comparison.

49. John Dunn, "The Claim to Freedom of Conscience: Freedom of Speech, Freedom of Thought, Freedom of Worship?" in *The History of Political Theory and Other Essays* (Cambridge, UK: Cambridge University Press, 1996), 100–120.

50. Goldie, ed., *A Letter Concerning Toleration*, 15.

CHAPTER TWO

1. Philip F. Gura, *A Glimpse of Sion's Glory: Puritan Radicalism in New England, 1620–1660* (Middletown, CT: Wesleyan University Press, 1984) provides a good introduction to this theme.

2. Richard W. Pointer, "Native Freedom? Indians and Religious Tolerance in Early America," in *The First Prejudice: Religious Tolerance and Intolerance in Early America*, ed. Chris Beneke and Christopher S. Grenda (Philadelphia: University of Pennsylvania Press, 2011), 169–194 offers a general introduction (quotation from Edwards at 174–175).

3. Jon Butler, *Awash in a Sea of Faith: Christianizing the American People* (Cambridge, MA: Harvard University Press, 1990), 43–45, 106–116.

4. Kenneth Lockridge, *A New England Town: The First Hundred Years, Dedham, Massachusetts, 1636–1736* (New York: W. W. Norton and Co., 1970).

5. David Hall, *Worlds of Wonder, Days of Judgment: Popular Religious Belief in Early New England* (Cambridge, MA: Harvard University Press, 1989), 4–5.

6. I refer here to Philip Greven's pioneering work in demographic and town history, *Four Generations: Population, Land, and Family in Colonial Andover, Massachusetts* (Ithaca, NY: Cornell University Press, 1970), and to my college classmate James West Davidson's great monograph, *The Logic of Millennial Thought* (New Haven, CT: Yale University Press, 1977), which brings a deft touch to a complex subject.

7. Edmund Morgan, *Visible Saints: The History of a Puritan Idea* (Ithaca, NY: Cornell University Press, 1963).

8. Morgan, *Visible Saints*, 64–80, for an account of the process of conversion.

9. Ibid., 93–112.

10. Robert G. Pope, *The Half-Way Covenant: Church Membership in Puritan New England* (Princeton, NJ: Princeton University Press, 1969) offers a pioneering account of this complicated process.

11. Gura, *A Glimpse of Sion's Glory*, 4–5.

12. Bejan, *Mere Civility*, 70–71.

13. It would be entirely fair to view the founding generation of Quakers as antecedents for twentieth-century Jehovah's Witnesses, those great litigants of religious liberty.

14. Susan Juster, *Sacred Violence in Early America* (Philadelphia: University of Pennsylvania Press, 2016), 182–183.

15. Evan Haefeli, *New Netherlands and the Dutch Origins of American Religious Liberty* (Philadelphia: University of Pennsylvania Press, 2012), 284.

16. Juster, *Sacred Violence*, 170–171; Locke, "Pennsylvania Laws," in Goldie, ed., *Letter Concerning Toleration*, 182.

17. Bejan, *Mere Civility*, 155, 141; Juster, *Sacred Violence*, 126–191.

18. Bernard Bailyn, *The Peopling of British North America: An Introduction* (New York: Alfred A. Knopf, 1985), 89–91, 112

19. Chris Beneke, *Beyond Toleration: The Religious Origins of American Pluralism* (New York: Oxford University Press, 2006), 17–48.

20. Sowerby, *Making Toleration*, 254–255.

21. Sally Schwartz, *"A Mixed Multitude": The Struggle for Toleration in Colonial Pennsylvania* (New York: New York University Press, 1987), 292–302 (summarizing the argument of an excellent book).

22. Ibid., 298–299.

23. James T. Lemon, *The Best Poor Man's Country: A Geographical Study of Early Southeastern Pennsylvania* (Baltimore: The Johns Hopkins University Press, 1972), xiii–xvi

24. It was, interestingly enough, the German vote (which was both Lutheran and Reformed) and the Scotch-Irish Presbyterians that helped to preserve the Penn family's proprietary rule in the crucial election of 1764, when Benjamin Franklin and his allies were desperately hoping to elect a coalition that favored turning Pennsylvania into a royal colony.

James H. Hutson, *Pennsylvania Politics, 1746–1770: The Movement for Royal Government and Its Consequences* (Princeton, NJ: Princeton University Press, 1972), 170–177.

25. This is extensively discussed in Schwartz, *"A Mixed Multitude,"* 159–256, and in numerous other works on the colony's history; and see especially Schwartz's concluding remarks at 250–256.

26. Frank Lambert, *Inventing the "Great Awakening"* (Princeton NJ: Princeton University Press, 1999); Jon Butler, "Enthusiasm Described and Decried: The Great Awakening as Interpretative Fiction," *Journal of American History* 69 (1982), 305–325.

27. Beneke, *Beyond Toleration*, 53. For more general treatments, see the great first book of Richard L. Bushman, *From Puritan to Yankee: Character and the Social Order in Connecticut, 1690–1765* (Cambridge, MA: Harvard University Press, 1967), 183–220.

28. For a moving account of the journey to hear Whitefield, see the opening passages of Michael J. Crawford, ed., "The Spiritual Travels of Nathan Cole," *William and Mary Quarterly* 3, no. 33 (1976), 89–126.

29. Douglas L. Winiarski, *Darkness Fall on the Land of Light: Experiencing Religious Awakenings in Eighteenth-Century New England* (Chapel Hill: University of North Carolina Press, 2017), provides a fascinatingly detailed and scrupulously documented accounted of this process.

30. Beneke, *Beyond Toleration*, 81–86 (quotation at 85–86).

31. Ibid., 87–112.

32. Beneke, *Beyond Toleration*, 119–125 offers an incisive (and ironic and even irenic) account of this controversy.

CHAPTER THREE

1. Bernard Bailyn, *The Ideological Origins of the American Revolution* (Cambridge, MA: Harvard University Press, 1967, 1992, 2017), 246–272.

2. Boyd, *Papers of Jefferson*, I: 548.

3. Ibid., viii.

4. Here I follow the lead of my colleague Caroline Winterer, *American Enlightenments: Pursuing Happiness in the Age of Reason* (New Haven, CT: Yale University Press, 2016).

5. Jefferson to Thomas Nelson, May 16, 1776, in Boyd, *Papers of Jefferson*, I: 292.

6. Jefferson to John Page, February 21, 1770, ibid., 34–35.

7. On these complicated matters, readers are advised to consult the rich work of Gideon Mailer, *John Witherspoon's American Revolution* (Chapel Hill: University of North Carolina Press, 2017). Chapter 8 of this book addresses "John Witherspoon, James Madison, and the American Founding."

8. Lance Banning, "James Madison, the Statute for Religious Freedom, and the Crisis of Republican Convictions," in *The Virginia Statute for Religious Freedom: Its Evolution and Consequences in American History*, ed. Merrill Peterson and Robert C. Vaughan (New York: Cambridge University Press, 1988), 109–110; and see Mailer, *Witherspoon's Revolution*, 332–340.

9. Madison to William Bradford, November 9, 1772, in William T. Hutchinson, William M. E. Rachal, et al., eds., *The Papers of James Madison* (Chicago and Charlottesville: University of Chicago Press and University of Virginia Press, 1962–), I: 74–75.

10. Madison to Bradford, January 23, 1774, ibid., 106.

11. Madison to Bradford, April 1, 1774, ibid., 112–113.

12. Boyd, ed., *Papers of Jefferson*, I: 363, 344, 353.

13. Beneke, *Beyond Toleration*, 133–135.

14. Notes on Episcopacy, Boyd, ed., *Papers of Jefferson*, I: 551–552.

15. Notes on Heresy, ibid., 553–555. To my regret, Jefferson did not explicitly discuss the Racovian catechism of the Socinians.

16. Here and in the paragraphs below, I draw upon the argument of Jack N. Rakove, *Declaring Rights: A Brief History in Documents* (Boston: Bedford Books, 1997).

17. For an editorial guide to the multiple versions and printings of the bill, see Julian Boyd's editorial note at *Papers of Jefferson*, II: 547–553. Because I am more concerned with the substance of Jefferson's ideas, rather than the legislative or printing history of the bill, I will rely on the 1779 text.

18. Peterson and Vaughan, *The Virginia Statute for Religious Freedom*.

19. *Notes on the State of Virginia*, Query XIII, in Merrill Peterson, ed., *Thomas Jefferson: Writings* (New York: Library of America, 1984), 246–251. On the significance of *quod leges*, see Jack N. Rakove, *Original Meanings: Politics and Ideas in the Making of the Constitution* (New York: Alfred A. Knopf, 1996), 94–108.

20. See the editorial note at *Papers of Madison*, VIII: 295–298 for the circumstances of its composition and circulation.

21. Michael McConnell, "The Origins and Historical Understanding of Free Exercise of Religion," *Harvard Law Review* 103 (1989–1990), 1449–1455 (quotation at 1453). We will return to this essay and McConnell's other writings in chapter 5.

22. *Notes on Virginia*, Query XVII, Peterson, *Jefferson: Writings*, 206.

23. Holly Brewer, *By Birth or Consent: Children, Law, and the Anglo-American Revolution in Authority* (Chapel Hill: University of North Carolina Press, 2005).

24. McConnell hedges his bets somewhat by conceding that "While [this passage] does not prove that Madison supported free exercise exemptions, it suggests an approach toward religious liberty consonant with them." *Consonant* is a very loose notion of historical intention, however; and the idea that "the dictates of religious faith must take precedence over the laws of the state, even if they are secular and generally applicable" is far more McConnell's conclusion than Madison's. McConnell, "Origins and Historical Understanding," 1453.

25. Knowingly or not, Madison was echoing the passage on religious liberty in *Notes on Virginia* where Jefferson fretted that "from the conclusion of this war we shall be going down hill." When it came to fixing rights, there was no substitute for the present.

26. Madison to Jefferson, January 22, 1786, Hutchinson et al., eds., *Papers of Madison*, VIII: 473–474.

27. Jefferson to Madison, December 16, 1786, ibid., IX: 211.

28. Madison to Caleb Wallace, August 23, 1785, ibid., VIII: 351; Madison to Jefferson, October 24, 1787, ibid., X: 212.

29. Essay on Property, March 27, 1792, ibid., XIV: 266–267. Here Madison was again following Locke, who had made the same point in his *Second Treatise*. Tee shirts inscribed "Conscience is the most sacred of all property" are available for purchase in the gift shop at James Madison's Montpelier. I wear mine regularly.

30. Vices of the Political System [April 1787], ibid., IX: 356.

31. Madison to Jefferson, October 17, 1788, ibid., XI: 297–299, for this and the following two paragraphs.

32. We assume too casually that a tacit bargain to add a bill of rights to the Constitution was an overt result of the ratification campaign of

1787–1788. In fact, a majority of congressmen, both Federalists and Anti-Federalists, had mixed feelings about this project, and Madison personally believed he was waging an uphill battle to force "the nauseous project of amendments" down the throats of a reluctant Congress. See Madison to Richard Peters, August 12, 1789, ibid., XII: 346.

33. Neil H. Cogan, ed., *The Complete Bill of Rights: The Drafts, Debates, Sources, and Origins* (New York: Oxford University Press, 1997), 1–11 traces the legislative history.

34. Madison to Nicholas P. Trist, May 1832, Rakove, ed., *Madison: Writings*, 860.

35. See Denise A. Spielberg, *Thomas Jefferson's Qur'an: Islam and the Founders* (New York: Alfred A. Knopf, 2013), 81–123.

36. For a general discussion, see Lynn Hunt, Margaret C. Jacob, and Wijnand Mijnhardt, *The Book That Changed Europe: Picart & Bernard's Religious Ceremonies of the World* (Cambridge, MA: Harvard University Press, 2010). Although Jefferson apparently did not own a copy of this influential work, he certainly belonged to the intellectual world it helped to shape.

37. J. G. A. Pocock, "Religious Freedom and the Desacralization of Politics," in Peterson and Vaughan, *Virginia Statute for Religious Freedom*, 66–70.

38. Madison to Robert Walsh, March 2, 1819, Rakove, *Madison: Writings*, 726–727.

CHAPTER FOUR

1. 98 U.S. 145 (1879).

2. On this point, see Lincoln A. Mullen, *The Chance of Salvation: A History of Conversion in America* (Cambridge, MA: Harvard University Press, 2017).

3. Nathan Hatch, *The Democratization of American Christianity* (New Haven, CT: Yale University Press, 1989), 3–5. For a contrasting view, see Amanda Porterfield, *Conceived in Doubt: Religion and Politics in the New American Nation* (Chicago: University of Chicago Press, 2012).

4. Sarah Barringer Gordon, "The First Disestablishment: Limits on Church Power and Property before the Civil War," *University of Pennsylvania*

*Law Review* 162 (2014), 307–312; for a more concise statement, see Gordon, "Religious Corporations and Disestablishment, 1780–1840," in *The Rise of Corporate Religious Liberty*, ed. Micah Schwartzman, Chad Flanders, and Zoë Robinson (New York: Oxford University Press, 2016), 63–76.

5. Sehat, *The Myth of American Religious Freedom*, 5; Green, *The Second Disestablishment*.

6. James C. Turner, *Philology: The Forgotten Origins of the Modern Humanities* (Princeton, NJ: Princeton University Press, 2014), 210–229 (quotation at 210).

7. Beneke, *Beyond Toleration*, 214–216.

8. Porterfield, *Conceived in Doubt*, 14–47, and more generally, Matthew Stewart, *Nature's God: The Heretical Origins of the American Republic* (New York: W. W. Norton and Co., 2014). Leigh Eric Schmidt, *Village Atheists: How America's Unbelievers Made Their Way in a Godly Nation* (Princeton, NJ: Princeton University Press, 2016), 1–24, although primarily concerned with the late nineteenth century, is also helpful on this point.

9. James C. Turner, *Without God, without Creed: The Origins of Unbelief in America* (Baltimore: The Johns Hopkins University Press, 1985), 43–49, 102.

10. Gordon, "The First Disestablishment," 317.

11. George Washington, Farewell Address, in John Rhodehamel, *George Washington: Writings* (New York: Library of America, 1997), 971; for Hamilton's draft, see Jacob Cooke and Harold Syrett, eds., *The Papers of Alexander Hamilton* (New York: Columbia University Press, 1962–1979), XX, 280. There is little evidence that Washington ever took any serious interest in religious reading; it is a topic conspicuously neglected in Kevin Hayes, *George Washington: A Life in Books* (New York: Oxford University Press, 2017).

12. George Washington to the Hebrew Congregation in Newport, [August 18, 1790], in W. W. Abbott, ed., *The Papers of George Washington: Presidential Series* (Charlottesville: University of Virginia Press, 1987–), VI: 284–286. The first sentence in the quotation echoes the congregation's letter; the second was the president's own composition, though he could have been assisted here by Secretary of State Jefferson, who accompanied the president on the trip. The next sentence, not quoted here, contains the phrase describing the American government as one "which gives to bigotry no sanction, to persecution no assistance" also originated in the congregation's address. See T. H. Breen, *George Washington's Journey: The President Forges a New Nation* (New York: Simon and Schuster, 2016), 202–206.

13. Hatch, *Democratization of American Christianity*, 49–58, 81–93, 133–141.

14. This point is well made in Christine Heyrman, *Southern Cross: The Beginnings of the Bible Belt* (New York: Alfred A. Knopf, 1997).

15. This characterization comes from Gordon S. Wood, "The Trials and Tribulations of Thomas Jefferson," in *Jeffersonian Legacies*, ed. Peter Onuf (Charlottesville: University of Virginia Press, 1993), 413.

16. Kellen Funk, "Church Corporations and the Conflict of Laws in Antebellum America," *Journal of Law and Religion* 32 (2017), 266–269; and see Mark Douglas McGarvie, *One Nation under Law: America's Early National Struggles to Separate Church and State* (DeKalb, IL: Northern Illinois University Press, 2004), 110–117.

17. 17 U.S. (4 Wheat.) 518 (1819).

18. McGarvie, *One Nation under Law*, 165–173, provides an excellent summary on which I have relied.

19. 10 U.S. (6 Cranch) 87 (1810).

20. 3 U.S. 43 (1815).

21. McGarvie, *One Nation under Law*, 173–182; Funk, "Church Corporations," 271–273.

22. 10 Paige 627 (N.Y. 1888).

23. Funk, "Church Corporations," 273–280 (quotations at 275, 279).

24. Gordon, "The First Disestablishment," 317–324.

25. Ibid., 311–312; Goldie, *A Letter Concerning Toleration*, 15 and n.31.

26. Gordon, "The First Disestablishment," 347–355 (quotation at 351).

27. 8 Johns. R. 290 (N.Y. 1811).

28. 37 Mass. 206 (1838).

29. Leonard Levy, *Blasphemy: Verbal Offense against the Sacred, from Moses to Salman Rushdie* (New York: Alfred A. Knopf, 1993), 400–423 (quotations at 400, 413).

30. Sehat, *Myth of American Religious Freedom*, 59–64.

31. John W. Compton, *The Evangelical Origins of the Living Constitution* (Cambridge, MA: Harvard University Press, 2014), 19–51; W. J. Rorabaugh, *The Alcoholic Republic: An American Tradition* (New York: Oxford University Press, 1979).

32. Compton, *Evangelical Origins*, 52–72.

33. James Madison, Speech of June 30, 1787, in Rakove, ed., *Madison: Writings*, 118. In her account of the compilation of his notes of

debates at Philadelphia, Mary Bilder questions whether Madison actually expressed these ideas on June 30, or incorporated them later as a mark of "his developing thoughts" on slavery. Mary Sarah Bilder, *Madison's Hand: Revising the Constitutional Convention*, (Cambridge, MA: Harvard University Press, 2015), 108.

34. Madison to Robert Walsh, November 27, 1819, in Rakove, ed., *Madison: Writings*, 744.

35. I rely here on Jud Campbell, "Testimonial Exclusions and Religious Freedom in Early America," *Law and History Review* 37 (2019), 431–492, which originated in part as a research paper for my seminar.

36. Green, *Second Disestablishment*, 251.

37. Ibid., 253–264.

38. 23 Ohio St. 211 (1872).

39. Green, *Second Disestablishment*, 275–276.

40. Ibid., 275–285; for the citation of the Farewell Address, see *The Bible in the Public Schools: Opinion and Decision of the Supreme Court of Ohio, in the Case of John D. Minor* Et al., *vs. The Board of Education of the City of Cincinnati* Et al. (Cincinnati, 1873), 226.

41. Green, *The Bible, the School, and the Constitution*, 118.

42. *The Bible in the Public Schools*, 243–245.

43. Ibid., 251–253.

44. Madison, Memorial and Remonstrance, item 11, in Rakove, ed., *Madison: Writings*, 34; *The Bible in the Public Schools*, 251.

45. Gordon S. Wood, "Evangelical America and Early Mormonism," *New York History* 61 (1980), 378–386 (quotation at 380).

46. David F. Holland, *Sacred Borders: Continuing Revelation and Canonical Restraint in Early America* (New York: Oxford University Press, 2011), 146–148.

47. Beneke, *Beyond Toleration*, 214–216.

48. Sarah Barringer Gordon, *The Mormon Question: Polygamy and Constitutional Conflict in Nineteenth-Century America* (Chapel Hill: University of North Carolina Press, 2002), 22–26. For an extremely helpful introduction to the complexities of Mormon historiography, see Jan Shipps, "Richard Lyman Bushman, the Story of Joseph Smith and Mormonism, and the New Mormon History," *Journal of American History* 94 (2007), 498–516.

49. Gordon, *The Mormon Question*, 26–27.

50. Ibid., 81–82.

51. Ibid., 85–92 (quotation at 87).

52. Ibid., 113–116.

53. 60 U.S. (19 How.) 393 (1857).

54. Ibid., 119–130.

55. *Reynolds v. U.S.*, 98 U.S. 145 (1879) at 162.

56. 98 U.S. 167.


CHAPTER FIVE


1. 23 Ohio St. 211 (1872).

2. 98 US 145 (1879).

3. Greenawalt, *Religion and the Constitution*, I.

4. 268 U.S. 510 (1925).

5. The best known are the Flag Salute cases of *Minersville School District v. Gobitis*, 310 U.S. 586 1940) and *West Virginia Board of Education v. Barnette*, 319 U.S. 624 (1943), but other leading decisions are equally important, notably including *Cantwell v. Connecticut*, 310 U.S. 296 (1940), *Chaplinsky v. New Hampshire*, 315 U.S. 568 (1942), and *Massachusetts v. Prince*, 321 U.S. 158 (1944). All but *Prince* will be discussed below.

6. 374 U.S. 398 (1963).

7. 406 U.S. 205 (1972).

8. 494 U.S. 872 (1990).

9. 521 U.S. 507 (1997).

10. 573 U.S. 682 (2014).

11. 508 U.S. 520 (1993).

12. 546 U.S. 418 (2006).

13. 584 U.S. ___ (2018).

14. *Holt v. Hobbs*, 574 U.S. 352 (2015) is the most important recent case. It concerned the length of a Muslim prisoner's beard.

15. "Gobitas" is the correct spelling of the family name, but the legal docket misspelled it as "Gobitis." Readers will find both spellings used hereafter, depending on context.

16. This paragraph and the entire succeeding section devoted to the Witnesses is deeply indebted to Shawn Francis Peters, *Judging Jehovah's Witnesses: Religious Persecution and the Dawn of the Rights Revolution* (Lawrence,

KS: University Press of Kansas, 2000), 19–45 (for the *Gobitis* case). It is worth noting that here (as elsewhere) state court actions are usually neglected in this realm of constitutional scholarship. For a healthy corrective on the flag salute cases, see Jeffrey S. Sutton, *51 Imperfect Solutions: States and the Making of American Constitutional Law* (New York: Oxford University Press, 2018), 133–172.

17. Peters, *Judging Jehovah's Witnesses*, 37. The manuscript can be viewed at the American Memory website of the Library of Congress.

18. 268 U.S. 652 (1925).

19. 310 U.S. 586 (1940).

20. Peters, *Judging Jehovah's Witnesses*, 46–60.

21. 310 U.S. 600.

22. 304 U.S. 144 (1938).

23. 310 U.S., at 605–606.

24. Peters, *Judging Jehovah's Witnesses*, 60–71.

25. See, in general, Elizabeth Kopelman Borgwardt, *A New Deal for the World: America's Vision for Human Rights* (Cambridge, MA: Harvard University Press, 2005).

26. Ronald Tsai, "Reconsidering *Gobitis*: An Exercise in Presidential Leadership," *Washington University Law Review*, 82 (2008), 400 (2008).

27. Ibid., 411. Cf. Victor Rotnem and F. G. Folsom Jr., "Recent Restrictions upon Religious Liberty," *American Political Science Review* 36 (1942), 1053–1068.

28. 319 U.S. 633–635. For this account, I rely chiefly on David M. Rabban, *Free Speech in Its Forgotten Years* (New York: Cambridge University Press, 1997), 342–380.

29. 319 U.S. 643–646.

30. Peters, *Judging Jehovah's Witnesses*, 52–60. One noteworthy aspect of these cases is how seriously they took the claims of the schoolchildren. They were treated not as passive conduits of their parents' influence or control but as morally autonomous actors, "children having a strong religious conviction" of their own. The moral value of protecting their liberty far outweighed the nebulous benefits of a momentary civic ritual.

31. Sarah Barringer Gordon, *The Spirit of the Law: Religious Voices and the Constitution in Modern America* (Cambridge, MA: Harvard University Press, 2010), 75.

32. 310 U.S. 296 (1940)

33. 310 U.S., at 303–307.
34. Peters, *Judging Jehovah's Witnesses*, 203–216.
35. 315 U.S. 568 (1942).
36. Ibid., at 571–573.
37. Here again I rely on Bejan, *Mere Civility*, 2–49.
38. Lupu and Tuttle, *Secular Government, Religious People* , 185.
39. Ibid., 188.
40. 366 U.S. 599 (1961).
41. Ibid., 603–607. Warren's language here reads like a textual rendering of a Normal Rockwell painting: "a day when the hectic tempo of everyday existence ceases and a more pleasant atmosphere is created, a day which all members of the family and community have the opportunity to spend and enjoy together, a day on which people may visit friends and relatives who are not available during working days, a day when the weekly laborer may best regenerate himself."
42. 366 U.S., 611–615.
43. *Sherbert v. Verner*, 374 U.S. 398, 404–406.
44. Lupu and Tuttle, *Secular Government, Religious People*, 192.
45. Nussbaum, *Liberty of Conscience*, 135–139.
46. *Wisconsin v. Yoder*, 406 U.S. 205, 218 (1972).
47. Ibid., at 219.
48. Ibid., at 221–225.
49. Ibid., at 242–243.
50. 393 U.S. 503 (1969).
51. 406 U.S., at 245–246.
52. Hamilton, *God vs. the Gavel*, 222.
53. Theodore Dwight Bozeman, *To Live Ancient Lives: The Primitivist Dimension in Puritanism* (Chapel Hill: University of North Carolina Press, 1988).
54. Marci A. Hamilton, "The Missing Children in Elite Legal Scholarship," in *The Conscience Wars: Rethinking the Balance between Religion, Identity, and Equality*, ed. Susanna Mancini and Michel Rosenfeld (New York: Oxford University Press, 2018), 366.
55. Jefferson to Peter Carr, September 7, 1814, in J. Jefferson Looney et al., eds., *The Papers of Thomas Jefferson: Retirement Series* (Princeton, NJ: Princeton University Press, 2010), VII: 637.

56. 406 U.S., at 247 n. 5 (quoting Justice Heffernan of the Wisconsin Supreme Court).

57. 485 U.S. 439 (1988).

58. See Justice Brennan's dissent, 485 U.S., at 465.

59. 461 U.S. 574 (1983)

60. 475 US 503 (1986).

61. Michael W. McConnell, "Accommodation of Religion," 1985 *Supreme Court Review* (1985) 3.

62. Michael McConnell, "The Origins and Historical Understanding of Free Exercise of Religion." *Harvard Law Review* 103 (1989–1990), 1409–1517, esp. 1449–1455.

63. McConnell was specifically concerned with two recent decisions of the Supreme Court *Wallace v. Jaffree*, 472 U.S. 38 (1985) (overturning an Alabama statute authorizing a minute-long period of silent meditation at the start of the school day); *Estate of Thornton v. Caldor, Inc.*, 472 U.S. 7903 (1985) (overturning a Connecticut statute giving employees an absolute right not to work on their Sabbath). As an assistant to the Solicitor General, McConnell had worked on both cases.

64. McConnell, *Accommodation of Religion*, 1.

65. Ibid., 14–24; quotations at 14 and 16.

66. Ibid., 15.

67. Ibid., at 19; Rakove, *Madison: Writings*, 78, 151.

68. For a retrospective assessment, see Tushnet, "*Accommodation of Religion* Thirty Years On."

69. McConnell, "Origins of Free Exercise," 1420.

70. 494 U.S. 872 (1990).

71. There are two excellent accounts of this case: Carolyn N. Long, *Religious Freedom and Indian Rights: The Case of* Oregon v. Smith (Lawrence, KS: University Press of Kansas, 2000); and Garrett Epps, *Peyote vs. the State: Religious Freedom on Trial* (Norman, OK: University of Oklahoma Press, 2009).

72. Long, *Religious Freedom*, 196–197.

73. Ibid., 137–147.

74. 494 U.S., at 887–888.

75. 494 U.S. 902–903.

76. Long, *Religious Freedom*, 205–211.

77. There is to my knowledge no adequate legislative history of the adoption of either the federal RFRA or its state-based complements. I have relied on the succinct account in Long, *Religious Freedom*, 203–250.

78. Ibid., 218–220, 228–231.

79. Lupu and Tuttle, *Secular Government, Religious People*, 226.

80. A helpful article here is James E. Ryan, "*Smith* and the Religious Freedom Restoration Act: An Iconoclastic Assessment," 78 *Virginia Law Review* 78 (1992), 1407–1462.

81. 521 U.S. 507 (1997).

82. Hamilton had articulated her position in "The Religious Freedom Restoration Act: Letting the Fox into the Henhouse under Cover of Section 5 of the Fourteenth Amendment," *Cardozo Law Review* 16 (1994), 357–398.

83. 521 U.S., at 519–520, 530.

84. 508 U.S. 520 (1993).

85. William Shakespeare, *Henry IV, Part I*, Act 3, Scene 1.

86. Ira C. Lupu, "*Hobby Lobby* and the Dubious Enterprise of Religious Exemptions," *Harvard Journal of Law and Gender* 38 (2015), 39–48 (quotation at 43).

87. 546 U.S. 418 (2006).

88. Lupu, "*Hobby Lobby* and Religious Exemptions," 62–75 (quotation at 73); and see Christopher Lund, "Religious Liberty after Gonzalez: A Look at State RFRAs," *South Dakota Law Review* 55 (2010), 466. Where Lupu is deeply skeptical of the RFRA regime, Lund openly favors its extension; yet here their assessments seem to coincide.

89. Madison to Edmund Pendleton, February 24, 1787, *Madison: Writings*, 62.

90. Frederick Mark Gedicks, "One Cheer for *Hobby Lobby*: Improbable Alternatives, Truly Strict Scrutiny, and Third-Party Employee Burdens," *Harvard Journal of Law and Gender* 38 (2015), 176.

91. Douglas Laycock, "The Campaign against Religious Liberty," in *The Rise of Corporate Religious Liberty*, ed. Micah Schwartzman, Chad Flaners, and Zoë Robinson (New York: Oxford University Press, 2016), 254–255.

92. Goldie, *A Letter Concerning Toleration*, 12–13.

93. McConnell, "Origins of Free Exercise," 1466. The much more comprehensive survey of these issues done by Ellis West reaches conclusions directly opposite to McConnell's. Ellis M. West, *The Free Exercise of Religion*

*in America: Its Original Constitutional Meaning* (Cham, Switzerland: Palgrave Macmillan, [2019]).

94. Douglas Nejaime and Reva B. Siegel, "Conscience Wars: Complicity-Based Conscience Claims in Religion and Politics," *Yale Law Journal* 124 (2015), 2518–2520.

95. To take one example: When Jews chant the *Al Chet* confession at their liturgy a tort of their sins would also be legally objectionable, but for the most part this collection of sins are acts against God and and one's own conscience.

96. See, for example, Nelson Tebbe, Micah Schwartzman, and Richard Schragger, "When Do Religious Accommodations Burden Others?" in *The Conscience Wars*, ed. Susanna Mancini and Michael Rosenfeld, 340–345.

97. For my most recent thoughts on this subject, see Rakove, "Politics Indoors and Out-of-Doors: A Fault Line in Madison's Thinking," in *The Cambridge Companion to* "The Federalist," ed. Jack Rakove and Colleen Sheehan (New York: Cambridge University Press, 2020), 370–399.

98. Mitchell Snay, *Gospel of Disunion: Religion and Separatism in the Antebellum South* 113–150 (Chapel Hill: University of North Carolina Press, 1997).

# Index

. . .

INDEX

Douglas, William O., 10–11, 147–48, 158, 159–61, 182–83
Dover, Treaty of (1670), 29–30
*Dred Scott v. Sandford* (1857), 169–70
Due Process Clause, Fourteenth Amendment, 142–43
Dunn, John, 38 39
Dutch Reformed Church, 53, 114

early American concepts of free exercise, 4–5, 7–8, 41–65
    conversion experience, importance of, 7–8, 41–42, 43–50
    denominational diversity, sources and impacts of, 49–56
    dissent becomes an anachronism, 56–65
    Dominion of New England and, 57–58
    Great Awakenings, xii–xiii, 7–9, 41–42, 49–50, 57, 61–65
    indigenous religious practice and, 43
    in Massachusetts, 42, 50–51, 52, 57–58
    in New York, 52–53, 55–56, 61
    in Pennsylvania, 54–56, 59–61
    religious freedom/toleration not an initial American value, 6–7, 14–15, 42–43
    in Rhode Island, 42, 52, 58
    sacralization of distinctive American landscape, 43–46
East India Company, 115–16
Edict of Nantes, revocation of (1685), xi–xii, 2, 18, 23–24, 32, 34
education
    Bible-reading in schools, 104–5, 123–29
    *Dartmouth College v. Woodward* (1819), 112–13
    Huguenot children and, 24
    Jefferson on public education, 82–83, 123–24, 158–59, 160–61
    Locke on, 39–40, 123, 161–62
    religious/parochial schools, public funding of, 123–24
Edwards, Jonathan, 43, 49–50
Elizabeth I (queen of England), 25–26, 191n22
England
    Civil War and Restoration, 27–29, 35, 191n22
    Exclusion Crisis (1678-1681), 54
    Glorious Revolution (1688), 25, 30–33, 58, 191n22
    religious toleration, development of regime of, 25–33

Enlightenment, 54, 57, 69, 97–98, 192–93n48
Episcopalians. *See* Church of England
equality and religious freedom, 84–85, 179–80, 183–84
*eruv,* 14
"Essay on Toleration" (Locke, 1667), 35–36
Establishment Clause, 95–96, 163, 186
establishment/disestablishment of religion. *See also* separation of church and state
    in colonial New England, 58
    in colonial Pennsylvania, 59–60
    deeper meaning of, 2–3
    law and governance, churches resorting to, 103–4, 111–17
    moral Protestant establishment, rise of, 8–9, 104–6
    in Pennsylvania constitution of 1790, 102
    radical US version of, 4–5
    revolutionary connection to free exercise, 68
    "second disestablishment," 8–9, 104, 132–33
    Virginia, establishment/disestablishment of Church of England in, 72–73, 75, 79, 80–87, 177–78
*Estate of Thornton v. Caldor, Inc.* (1985), 205n63
European regime of religious toleration, 6–7, 13–40
    between Christian denominations, 16, 22
    communal practices, moderating mechanisms, and confessional tendencies, 19–25
    defining tolerance and toleration, 13–14
    doctrinal origins of intolerance, 16–17
    England's development of, 25–33
    infidels, Jews, Moslems, and indigenous American peoples, treatment of, 15–16, 22
    Locke's concept of toleration, 33–40
    philosophical advocates of tolerance, 16–19, 25
    *politique,* 18, 38
    as privilege versus right, 18
evangelical Protestantism, 8–9, 98, 117–18, 119–22, 175, 182–83
Exclusion Crisis (1678-1681), 54
exemptions and accommodations, 153–62, 179
*Federalist, The* 81
    10, 67–68, 70–71, 94–95, 98–99, 181–82
    37, 96
    51, 67–68, 98–99, 121, 181–82

[ 212 ]